Improving Primary Mathematics

Improving Primary Mathematics: Linking home and school provides primary teachers with practical ideas on how to bring these two worlds closer to improve children's mathematics learning. Using a number of fascinating case studies focusing on children's experiences of mathematics both inside and outside the classroom, the book asks:

- How do children use mathematics in their everyday lives?
- How can teachers use this knowledge to improve children's learning in school?
- What activities can teachers use with parents to help share the ways that schools teach mathematics?
- What can parents do to support their children's learning of mathematics?

Tried-and-tested practical suggestions for activities to support and encourage children's learning of mathematics include: making videos to share teaching methods; children taking photos to show how they use mathematics at home; inviting parents into school to share in mathematics learning; and numeracy-based activities for children and their parents to do together at home.

All those involved in planning, teaching and supporting primary mathematics will benefit from new insights into how learning at home and at school can be brought together to strengthen and improve children's learning of mathematics.

Jan Winter is Senior Lecturer in Education (Mathematics) and PGCE Course Director, University of Bristol, UK.

Jane Andrews is Senior Lecturer in Early Childhood Education, University of the West of England, UK.

Pamela Greenhough is Research Fellow at the Graduate School of Education, University of Bristol, UK.

Martin Hughes is Professor at the Graduate School of Education, University of Bristol, UK.

Leida Salway is a primary school teacher in Cardiff and worked for three years as a teacher researcher on the Home–School Knowledge Exchange Project.

Wan Ching Yee is Research Fellow at the Graduate School of Education, University of Bristol, UK.

TLRP Improving Practice Series

Series Editor: Andrew Pollard, Director of the ESRC Teaching and Learning Programme

Learning How to Learn: Tools for schools
Mary James, Paul Black, Patrick Carmichael, Colin Conner, Peter Dudley, Alison Fox, David Frost, Leslie Honour, John MacBeath, Robert McCormick, Bethan Marshall, David Pedder, Richard Procter, Sue Swaffield and Dylan Wiliam

Improving Primary Mathematics: Linking home and school
Jan Winter, Jane Andrews, Pamela Greenhough, Martin Hughes, Leida Salway and Wan Ching Yee

Improving Primary Literacy: Linking home and school
Anthony Feiler, Jane Andrews, Pamela Greenhough, Martin Hughes, David Johnson, Mary Scanlan and Wan Ching Yee

Improving Primary Mathematics

Linking home and school

Jan Winter, Jane Andrews,
Pamela Greenhough, Martin Hughes,
Leida Salway and Wan Ching Yee

Routledge
Taylor & Francis Group

LONDON AND NEW YORK

First published 2009
by Routledge
2 Park Square, Milton Park, Abingdon, Oxon OX14 4RN

Simultaneously published in the USA and Canada
by Routledge
270 Madison Avenue, New York, NY 10016

Routledge is an imprint of the Taylor & Francis Group, an informa business

© 2009 Jan Winter, Jane Andrews, Pamela Greenhough, Martin Hughes,
Leida Salway and Wan Ching Yee

Typeset in Melior and Futura by
Keystroke, 28 High Street, Tettenhall, Wolverhampton
Printed and bound in Great Britain by
MPG Books Ltd, Bodmin

British Library Cataloguing in Publication Data
A catalogue record for this book is available from the British Library

Library of Congress Cataloging in Publication Data
Improving primary mathematics : linking home and school / Jan Winter ... [et al.].
p. cm. – (Improving practice series)
Includes bibliographical references and index.
1. Mathematics–Study and teaching (Primary) 2. Mathematics–Study and
teaching–Parent participation. 3. Education, Primary–Parent participation.
4. Home schooling. I. Winter, Jan, 1956–
QA135.6.I476 2009
372.7–dc22
2008038200

ISBN 10: 0–415–36393–4 (pbk)
ISBN 10: 0–203–01513–4 (ebk)

ISBN 13: 978–0–415–36393–8 (pbk)
ISBN 13: 978–0–203–01513–1 (ebk)

Contents

Series preface

The ideas for *Improving Practice* contained in this book are underpinned by high quality research from the Teaching and Learning Research Programme (TLRP), the UK's largest ever coordinated investment in education enquiry. Each suggestion has been tried and tested with experienced practitioners and has been found to improve learning outcomes – particularly if the underlying principles about Teaching and Learning have been understood. The key, then, remains the exercise of professional judgement, knowledge and skill. We hope that the *Improving Practice* series will encourage and support teachers in exploring new ways of enhancing learning experiences and improving educational outcomes of all sorts. For future information about TLRP and additional 'practitioner applications', see www.tlrp.org.

Preface

This book – like its companion volume *Improving Primary Literacy: Linking home and school* (2007) – arose from the Home–School Knowledge Exchange Project, a research project based at the Graduate School of Education, University of Bristol. Details of the project are presented in the Appendix.

The project team was large, and the authors of this book had different roles within the team. Jan Winter led the numeracy strand of the project. Leida Salway was the teacher-researcher responsible for developing and implementing home–school mathematics activities; Pamela Greenhough was the leader of the project outcomes team, whose other members were Jane Andrews and Wan Ching Yee; and Martin Hughes was the overall project director.

(Throughout this book we use the term *mathematics* rather than *numeracy*. Although the term *numeracy* has been widely used in schools in recent years, it is now much more common to use *mathematics* and we also wish to indicate the broad approach we are taking to the ideas and activities involved in the subject.)

For each chapter, one member of the team took the lead in preparing initial drafts, as follows:

Chapter 1:   Martin Hughes
Chapter 2:   Jan Winter
Chapter 3:   Martin Hughes
Chapters 4 and 5:   Leida Salway
Chapter 6   Jan Winter

Wan Ching Yee and Jane Andrews provided case study material for Chapters 2 and 3, and were involved in evaluating the activities described in Chapters 4 and 5. Pamela Greenhough redrafted Chapter 2, to include the parents' views on their own mathematics learning, and redrafted Chapters 4 and 5, so that the activities are presented in the same format as in *Improving Primary Literacy*. In addition, Jan Winter and Martin Hughes carried out an overall edit of the draft chapters, aiming to provide coherence while allowing the different voices of the authors to come through.

There are strong links between this book and *Improving Primary Literacy* because the two books arose from strands of the same research project. While the curriculum areas led to different approaches being taken in project activities, we felt it would be helpful to readers if we structured the books in a similar way.

Finally, please note that we use the term 'parents' throughout the book as shorthand for 'parents and carers'.

Acknowledgements

The Home–School Knowledge Exchange Project was funded by the Economic and Social Research Council (ref no. L139 25 1078) as part of its Teaching and Learning Research Programme. We are very grateful to the Local Education Authorities of Bristol and Cardiff for their support, and to the many teachers, parents and children who took part in the project. We have used pseudonyms throughout the book and changed some details in order to protect the anonymity of the project participants. We would also like to thank the other members of the project team – Anthony Feiler, David Johnson, Elizabeth McNess, Marilyn Osborn, Andrew Pollard, Mary Scanlan and Vicki Stinchcombe; our project consultants – John Bastiani, Guy Claxton and Harvey Goldstein; and our project secretary Stephanie Burke.

Chapter 1

Why link home and school learning?

This book is about the different ways in which children learn and use mathematics at home and at school. It is also about how these different ways of mathematics learning can be brought more closely together, for the benefit of teachers, parents and children. The early chapters provide detailed accounts of school and home mathematics learning as experienced by a small group of children, and also recount the school mathematics experiences of these children's parents. The later chapters provide practical examples of activities designed to bring home and school mathematics learning more closely together, through a process of *home–school knowledge exchange*. We hope that readers of the book will gain new insights into the nature of mathematics learning, and come to understand why home–school knowledge exchange is so important. We also hope that readers will try out some of the knowledge exchange activities for themselves, and invent new ones which are tailored to their own particular circumstances.

Two key ideas about children's learning

This book, and its companion volume *Improving Primary Literacy: Linking home and school* (2007), are based on two fundamental ideas about children's learning and how it can be enhanced.

The first key idea is that children live and learn in two different worlds – home and school. Clearly, this is an idea that no one would seriously take issue with. Yet it is also one whose importance has never been fully accepted. When educators and politicians talk, as they frequently do, about the need to improve levels of children's mathematical attainment, they are usually advocating changes to the way children are taught mathematics in school. This kind of mathematics learning is of course very important: there is no doubt that much of what children learn about mathematics takes place through their lessons in school. But school is not the only place where mathematics learning goes on. As we shall see in Chapter 3, children are also learning about mathematics through their ongoing daily activities at home and in the wider community, as they interact with parents, grandparents, siblings and friends, and as they play games or help with everyday household activities such as cooking and shopping. This kind of learning is often hidden from public view, but it is of vital importance in understanding how children learn mathematics.

One consequence of children living and learning in two different worlds is that the two kinds of learning may become separated. Children may be unable or unwilling to draw on what they have learned in one world when they are in the other. The knowledge, skills and understanding they have acquired at school may not be accessible to them at home, and vice versa. Moreover, key adults who might be able to help children make the necessary connections between the two kinds of learning may not have sufficient knowledge to do so. Teachers may not know enough about what their children are learning at home, while parents may not know enough about what their children are learning at school.

In the area of mathematics, this kind of separation seems to be particularly acute at the moment. In England, the teaching of school mathematics has been transformed in recent years by the National Numeracy Strategy (now the Primary Framework for Mathematics. See www.standards.dfes.gov.uk/primaryframeworks/). While Wales has its own curriculum, broadly similar changes have happened there too, as local authorities have been responsible for introducing strategies to improve achievement in numeracy (Jones, 2002). The mathematics curriculum, the shape, content and pace of mathematics lessons, and the way that mathematics is assessed are all very different from how many of today's parents were taught. As a result, parents may not feel sufficiently confident to help their children at home, or worry that they might be confusing their children if they try to do so. Similarly, the nature of many children's out-of-school lives, and the kinds of mathematical procedures used at home, may be relatively opaque to their teachers, particularly when the children come from a different ethnic or religious community from that of their teacher.

This brings us to our second key idea – that *children's learning will be enhanced if home and school learning are brought more closely together*. Again, this appears to be an idea that few would take serious issue with. Teachers have long been encouraged to draw on children's out-of-school interests in their teaching, and to keep parents involved with and informed about their children's learning in school. Parents have long been encouraged to support their children's school learning at home. And indeed, there have been several influential research projects – some going back to the 1970s – which have demonstrated the value of parents and teachers working together to support children's learning, particularly in the area of mathematics. See for example, the IMPACT project which offered innovative ideas to engage both parents and children in mathematics homework (Merttens and Vass, 1990) and the Ocean maths project (www.ocean-maths.org.uk), a project in East London which works to encourage parents' involvement in their children's learning of mathematics.

As with our first key idea, though, the importance of this second idea has never been fully accepted. Teachers and headteachers often tell us that the pressure they are currently under to 'raise standards' means that developing effective home–school partnerships is, for many of them, an area of relatively low priority. We would reply that the most effective way to raise standards is to bring together children's home and school learning. These are not two competing priorities: rather, one is the means to the other.

There are signs, however, that things are changing. The recent *Review of Mathematics Teaching in Primary Schools and Early Years Settings* by Sir Peter Williams (Williams, 2008) concluded that:

> It is self-evident that parents are central to their child's life, development and attainment. They cannot be ignored or sidelined but should be a critical element in any practitioners' plans for the education of children.
>
> (para. 265)

The Review commented positively on the work of the Home–School Knowledge Exchange Project and specifically recommended that:

> teachers need to recognise the wealth of mathematical knowledge children pick up outside of the classroom, and help children to make links between 'in-school' and 'out-of-school' mathematics.
>
> (para. 257)

This book will provide practical examples of ways in which these links can be made.

The nature of the book

Improving Primary Mathematics arises directly from the Home–School Knowledge Exchange Project, which took place between 2001 and 2006. During this time we worked closely with teachers, parents and children from different communities in the two cities of Bristol and Cardiff, developing, implementing and evaluating a range of home–school knowledge exchange activities. We also carried out in-depth interviews with many of these teachers, parents and children, and asked parents and children to make video recordings of their home learning.

One strand of the project focused on home and school mathematics learning for children in Years 4 and 5, and the book draws heavily on the work of that strand. At the same time, it is not intended to be a full account of the research and its findings (see the Appendix for more details of the project). Rather, it is an attempt to make project outcomes available in a usable form to all those interested in children's mathematics learning – at all ages – and how it might be enhanced through home–school knowledge exchange. This includes:

- teachers
- headteachers
- numeracy coordinators and mathematics specialists
- family learning coordinators
- teaching assistants and learning support assistants
- students in initial training
- teachers on post-graduate courses
- teacher educators and other educationalists
- school governors
- parents and parents' organisations.

In order to make the contents of the book accessible to such a wide range of audiences we have deliberately emphasised practical action and the issues arising, and kept references to academic texts to a minimum. Readers are encouraged to try out and adapt the activities described here, and are free to photocopy and use the various sheets included in the text.

Chapter 2

Mathematics at school

The teaching of mathematics in English and Welsh primary schools has changed dramatically over the last ten years. Whether these changes have led to improved levels of achievement is very much open to debate [📖 Reading 2.1]. What is clear, however, is that many parents may not be familiar with the way mathematics teaching has changed or the rationale behind these changes. As a result, they may lack the confidence or knowledge to help their children with mathematics at home.

In this chapter we look at some school mathematics lessons involving four children – Olivia, Ryan, Nadia and Saqib. These children attended four contrasting primary schools in Bristol and Cardiff which participated in the Home–School Knowledge Exchange Project (see Appendix for more details). We start by looking at what these children's parents recall of their own experiences of learning mathematics at school. This will help us understand how they might see their children's current experiences of school mathematics.

Olivia's mother and school mathematics

Olivia's mother did not have good memories of learning mathematics at school:

> I disliked maths so much . . . and I was so useless at it, and told I was so useless at it. I've got a real dislike for it, you know, it's a bit of a phobia really, you know, because you think 'well I'm no good at that so I can't do that', whereas Olivia is so good at it and quite confident, that, you know, that's what makes it a little bit scary to a point – she's only eight and a half, you know, and she knows all that already.

Like many parents, Olivia's mother particularly remembered being taught multiplication. She was made to learn multiplication tables 'parrot fashion', and this experience was the start of her loss of confidence in mathematics:

> Oh, it was horrific, it was horrible . . . we used to have chalk thrown at us and things for getting it wrong and be humiliated in the classroom by being asked to stand up and say your times table. And if you got it wrong, repeating it until you said it, time and time again, and then, you know, by then my blush gland had been in overdrive and I'd be a ball of sweat and a bag of nerves. So [from] there on it went downhill really, right through my secondary education.

Olivia's mother thought that her lack of confidence and ability in mathematics had prevented her from qualifying as a nurse. When asked if she used mathematics in her current job in management, she said:

> Not very often. I mean we only use them, well, for budgets, managing budgets, but I use a calculator *[laughs]*. And you know it's very simple, when you've got

a calculator it's very easy, isn't it? So yeah, I don't need it, you know, I do a lot of ratios which is proportioning staff to service users but those are figures I can do in my head and do that quite confidently, because they're small, and you start giving me things up in the thousands and I think 'oh no, you know, I can't do it'.

Olivia's mother felt that the methods which Olivia was currently taught for mathematical procedures were different from those which she had been taught:

What confuses me is that they do their calculations slightly different to how we were taught to do them, and she came home this week and told me that she had learned to divide . . . because I try and show her my way and she says 'oh you don't know what you're doing' *[laughs]* . . . 'you have to section it' and I'm thinking 'oh no, I can't do that', you know. I probably could if I sat down with her, but she panics me a bit when she starts saying 'no, you're doing it wrong', because I know the way that I'm doing it will get the right answer, the same as hers – but it's going through the process of showing her how to do it.

Ryan's mother and school mathematics

Ryan's mother was brought up in Scotland and attended school there. Like Olivia's mother, Ryan's mother remembered learning her multiplication tables, although in her case this was by no means a traumatic experience:

Interviewer: Can you remember at Ryan's age, doing maths at that age?
Ryan's mother: Yeah, I was good at my tables – I could do them backwards, frontwards – I was really good.
Interviewer: Can you remember what they did to help you learn the tables?
Ryan's mother: You had blocks, you had to count your blocks . . . just say them, every time you went to maths. You would say a table, you would learn just about that table, five times table, and you would learn that – and you would learn it backwards as well. And just things like that, I would say.

However, while Ryan's mother felt she was good at multiplication, she struggled with division:

It was just the division, I couldn't do it . . . I just couldn't grasp it. I can remember the teacher sitting down and showing me how to do it – Miss X, her name was – and I just couldn't grasp it, it just would not sink in. I think that's where Ryan gets it from. But my tables and that, I'm really good.

Like Olivia's mother, Ryan's mother was aware that the methods her child was taught for calculations were different from the ones which she herself had been taught. As a result, she found it hard to help him with school work which he brought home, and it frequently led to arguments between them:

Ryan's mother: He's brought some maths home before and I'm no too bad at maths, but some . . . I don't know if it's just the way they pronounce some things and he's explaining it to me and I just haven't a clue and I just can't help him. With reading, yeah, I can help him, but when he's like working at sums and things like that . . . I'm no that thick like, but when it comes to doing like . . . oh, what do they call it *[pause]* it's like you've got to figure out the meaning of something and to get the answer . . . I can read it out to him, but he always says I'm wrong because I'm no doing it properly . . . and we end up at loggerheads.
Interviewer: So do you think that you *are* doing it a different way?

Ryan's mother: Oh, definitely. I had . . . see that's when I went to a meeting, the other week about the maths and everything. It's like you'll do your take-away sum . . . we used to do ten to the top, ten to the bottom. And she showed me, the teacher – you take one off the eight, it was, and it came as seven, and you put that on there, the others. It was entirely different.

In Chapter 3 we will see an example of Ryan and his mother being 'at loggerheads' as she tries to help him with some maths homework.

Nadia's father and school mathematics

Nadia's father attended school in Bangladesh, coming to England when he was 15. He recalled that there were few calculators around when he was at school, and he had to learn to do calculations using his fingers and his brain:

> But when we was in school in our time, my time, only few calculator had, you know, other way we have to do it on our fingers. . . . So, when we was in school in our time, my time, when I was a young kid – but that was about thirty-four, thirty-three years ago. So when I was seven, eight years old, so we used to use our brain, you know. There wasn't any calculator in our time.

Nadia's father used mathematics a lot in his job as manager of a restaurant. He said that for large calculations he used a computer, but most of the time he 'uses his brain':

> I feel more comfortable with the – more confidence in my brain – other than a calculator.

Nadia's father also stressed the importance of being competent with mathematics:

> If you go to work, you need maths. If you do any DIY, you need maths. If you go to bank, it's maths. Everywhere you need maths. Without mathematics you cannot live in this country. You get cheated.

Saqib's mother and school mathematics

Saqib's mother attended elementary school in Pakistan before moving to the UK. She did not speak much English and found it difficult to be interviewed in English. Talking through an interpreter, she explained how this limited her ability to help her children with their school mathematics:

Saqib's mother: The simple questions I understand because it's adding, subtracting, multiplication. But when it's a question written in English, I don't understand. I've studied maths up to 6 or 7 class – junior/infants, isn't it? But after that I didn't go to school but I was taught how to do basic maths. I've been here thirteen years and I've learnt a lot even in that time. Things have changed back home now. My younger sisters are doing very well in English and maths.

Interviewer: Are they here or back in Pakistan?

Saqib's mother: Pakistan. I feel very bad that I've missed out on that. They're doing quite well nowadays you know about maths. It's very important to learn maths, it's their future. I want my children to learn what I missed out on.

Later Saqib's mother expanded on how her own confidence and ability with mathematics had developed since she arrived in the UK. The interpreter explained:

> What mum is saying is that the early days were very, very difficult. But over the years she's picked up maths and English and now she's very confident. [Her

husband] is sometimes away for three months and when she's on her own she really has to stick to a budget . . . the income isn't regular, but she has to manage on the budget because with the school holidays the kids need a lot more – food and clothing, and they want the food of their choice – but mum has got to budget that money because now that school is re-opening they need everything.

Parents' recollections and their children's experiences

The parents of Olivia, Ryan, Nadia and Saqib provide a range of recollections of their own experiences of school mathematics. But while different, the recollections of these four parents are not untypical of many parents whom we interviewed in our research.

Some parents had memories similar to Olivia's mother of being embarrassed or humiliated in their mathematics lessons. Laura's mother, for example, remembered doing mental arithmetic around the class as a 'nightmare' which she used to 'dread'. Other parents resembled Ryan's mother in revealing a lack of understanding in particular areas – such as multiplication, division or fractions – which had left them unable or unwilling to help their children with mathematics. Not all experiences were negative, however. Phillip's mother talked with pleasure about a particular teacher who used to make lessons interesting and relevant by bringing in produce from his allotment – 'we used to do the maths lesson with gooseberries and then we could eat the gooseberries'. Other parents, who like Saqib's mother and Nadia's father had been educated outside the UK, wished they had received more than a very basic education, or that they had been taught by the same methods their children were now using. As Rajinder's mother said '[I know] my own Indian ways. I always tell her "I haven't been schooled in here, so I don't know in your way, but I can tell my way". I wish I went to school here, but I didn't'.

Drawing on the recollections of these and other parents, we provide a list in Box 2.1 of ways in which parents' experiences of learning mathematics may be different from the present-day experiences of their children. This list may be worth bearing in mind when considering the descriptions we now provide of recent mathematics lessons experienced by Olivia, Ryan, Nadia and Saqib. The curriculum context for these lessons is the National Numeracy Strategy, and the lessons all took place during Year 5, when the children were aged 9 or 10.

Box 2.1

Aspects of mathematics teaching which parents feel might have changed since their schooldays

- What counts as 'mathematics'
- Whether it's called 'mathematics' or 'numeracy'
- Classroom organisation
- Lesson organisation
- Teaching methods
- Strategies and procedures for carrying out calculations
- Equipment and materials used
- Measures used
- What mathematics children are expected to know at different ages
- Use of technology, such as calculators
- What counts as error, and the penalty for error.

Olivia and the fractions lesson

In Olivia's school, the mathematics groups are 'set' for some lessons – that is, the whole of the year group is split into groups, according to their achievement in mathematics. Olivia is in the 'top' group for the highest achievers. At the start of the lesson, the children are sitting at tables, facing the front. The teacher asks a series of quick-fire questions, such as:

> What is half of 12?
> Write down a third of 60.

Each child has to work out the answer in their heads and then write it on a small whiteboard. Olivia appears quite confident in answering, but sometimes she looks around her to check if her answer is the same as others' before she holds up her whiteboard for the teacher to see. The teacher can see all the children's answers at once, and she responds accordingly. The children then wipe off their answers, ready for the next calculation.

At one point the teacher has the following dialogue with one of Olivia's class-mates:

Teacher: How are you doing these?
Pupil: If you say 'a third', I divide by three; 'half', I divide by two; 'quarter', by four.
Teacher: What is a fraction of a whole?
Pupil: It's a part.

The teacher continues with questions, such as:

> What is a fifth of 20?
> Write down a ninth of 27.
> What is four-tenths of 200?

The work moves quickly. Olivia is not the quickest in the class, but she is always attentive and involved.

Next comes an exercise in which the children work in pairs on twenty fraction calculations written on identical cards. The children work together on each calculation, discussing what they think the answer might be. Before they start, the teacher asks the class to estimate how long the task will take them. Their estimates range from one minute to twenty minutes. The teacher says:

> See if you can do them in five minutes. I hope you're revving your brains up!

The fastest pair actually finish in 35 seconds, while Olivia and her partner take one minute and 25 seconds. The teacher asks the class:

> Was your estimate accurate? Did you underestimate how good you are at maths? You should be setting yourself challenges.

The teacher asks the pupils for their answers. Nearly all the children, including Olivia and her partner, have got them all right. The teacher asks the class:

> What way did I use to check if the answer was right or not?

One pupil suggests she used the 'inverse operation', and the teacher agrees that she could use multiplying to check whether the answers were correct.

The lesson moves on to fractions of various quantities – money, length, time, etc. One question is 'What fraction of £1 is 33p?' and most children either answer $^{33}/_{100}$ or $^1/_3$. When challenged to explain the latter answer, some recognise this is an approximate answer. Another question is 'What fraction of 1kg is 300g?' Olivia writes $^{300}/_{1000}$ but her teacher suggests she can make it smaller: other pupils have written $^3/_{10}$. The teacher says:

> Did anyone do it a different way? I thought – '100 grams is one tenth, so 300 grams must be three tenths' – that's just another way.

The last part of the lesson moves into conversions between fractions and decimals. The teacher asks pupils to convert some 'easy' fractions first, such as $^1/_2$ and $^1/_4$, but then gives them $^1/_3$ as a challenge. Some children are thrown by this, others suggest 0.333, and even 0.3 recurring. The teacher shows recurring decimal notation to the class, but does not explore it further. She goes on to include examples with mixed numbers (e.g. 3 $^3/_4$) and looks at why $^{89}/_{100}$ is the same as $^{890}/_{1000}$.

The children move on to work in pairs again, using cards handed out by the teacher. The blue cards have fractions on for converting into decimals, while for the red cards it is vice versa. Olivia's table have blue cards and she attempts to convert numbers such as 8 $^3/_{10}$ and $^{24}/_{10}$. For $^1/_5$ she writes '0.5' which she is able to correct to 0.2 when the teacher talks to her about it.

For the final exercise the children are given individual worksheets which require them to match fractions and decimals, joining them with a line. Olivia writes her name on the sheet and joins up the fractions and decimals carefully using a ruler. The bell goes for the end of the lesson and the sheets are collected in by a pupil.

Reflections on the fractions lesson

This lesson contains a number of features which are characteristic of mathematics classes since the National Numeracy Strategy was introduced in 1998 and which may be different from parents' experiences of their own mathematics learning. These include:

- The *interactive* nature of the work: almost all the lesson is spent with pupils working with the teacher or with one another – they have no time to work for a protracted period on their own.
- The *pace* of the work: a lot of ground is covered quickly and in a challenging way. Indeed at times the teacher gives the impression that the speed with which tasks are completed is more important than accuracy [📖 Reading 2.2].
- The *focus on mental methods:* children are expected to work out answers in their heads, using whatever methods they think are appropriate. At one point the teacher explicitly models the method she has used, suggesting that no single method is being imposed on the class.
- The use of *individual whiteboards*: these allow children to write and display their answers so the teacher gets an immediate sense of how many children are correct. At the same time much of the lesson becomes lost as answers are wiped off, so that looking in books will not give parents an accurate impression of what the children have done.

Olivia's teacher told us that she found the new methods challenging but felt they were successful. She talked about the importance of keeping the lessons both interactive and highly paced:

It's just constantly keeping them moving. Pushing them forward all the time and not letting them lose concentration, and so it kind of does fit in but you've got to be really strict. I find I've got to be really strict on time spans and be constantly going at them the whole time – and it has to be an interactive thing between us together, all the time. It's quite exhausting, but it's worth it, because they are learning and they have made progress.

Ryan and the percentages lesson

Ryan attends a primary school in Cardiff. Although the National Numeracy Strategy is not applicable to Wales, his school uses a very similar approach to teaching mathematics.

At the start of the lesson, Ryan is helping his teacher unravel the OHP lead. The teacher puts a transparency of a 100-square grid on the OHP and Ryan adjusts it – he seems to be the unofficial class technician. The children sit at tables facing the teacher and the OHP.

The topic of the lesson is percentages. The lesson begins with a 'question and answer' session recapping the previous day's content. The teacher asks the class about the previous lesson, and a pupil offers 'We were learning percentages'. The teacher asks 'linked to . . . ?' and the pupil answers 'decimals and fractions'. The teacher then proceeds to ask the class questions about percentages, using the 100-square grid as a concrete aid. At one point she asks Ryan to colour in 5% of the grid, which he does successfully. She asks 'Who can make it up to 15%?' and another child does so.

The lesson moves on quickly from percentages of a square to percentages of amounts. Pupils from all around the class are involved, putting their hands up to offer answers and being asked to explain their reasoning when they do. At one point the teacher asks for '50% of 82?' Ryan puts his hand up, and when he is nominated says '42'. The teacher repeats questioningly '42?' and Ryan corrects himself to '41'.

The questioning is at a very fast pace, gradually increasing the challenge of the percentages asked for. Some children become quieter and may be finding it difficult to follow the pace. The teacher asks questions about 25% and then 75% of amounts. She explains that 'for 75% you can find 25%, or a quarter, and multiply it by three'. She asks if anyone is confused, and Ryan puts up his hand, along with others. Ryan seems disengaged and is yawning at this point.

Soon the class breaks up into smaller groups. The children are given individual worksheets on percentages and the teacher goes round helping individuals. Ryan gets a pile of books to hand out and he distributes them to other children. He asks the teacher if he can help with the OHP, and then winds up the lead, rather than getting started on the worksheet.

The teacher comes to Ryan's table to check that they have all started work. Ryan asks 'Can I do a harder one?' but his teacher replies 'It's the same'. Ryan retorts 'It's not' but seems to accept the answer. However he soon returns to the OHP, unwinding and rewinding the lead. He works slowly and distractedly at the worksheet. When the teacher comes back to his table she looks at his book and says:

T: Good – what's 100% of 123?
Ryan: [tentatively] 123?
T: 100% is all of something and 50% is . . . ?
Ryan: [seems to guess] 21?
         [Another pupil gives the correct answer].
T: Yes, brilliant!
         [A few minutes later they have another exchange]:
Ryan: Miss, Miss!

T:	What are you stuck on? If I've got 20 and I want to find a quarter, what should I do?
Ryan:	100 something.
T:	A quarter.
Ryan:	300 and . . .
T:	If you want a quarter of the pie how many pieces should I give you?
Ryan:	*[hesitates, but doesn't answer]*
T:	If I divide a square into four – do you have a pencil? Oh, it doesn't work – you divide this into quarters for me. Yeah, how many pieces?
Ryan:	Four.
T:	Now colour in four. *[Ryan does]* Excellent! So if we want a quarter of a number, how do we do it? We divide by how many?
Ryan:	Four.
T:	If we have 20 divided by four?
Ryan:	30.
T:	Five isn't it? So five is one quarter of 20, that's all you're doing. So where it's got 25%, divide by four. So if you've got 400 pieces in our pie, and you want to divide it between four of us – how many is each bit?
Ryan:	Four.
T:	One quarter is how much?
Ryan:	100.
T:	25% is the same as dividing by four – you can do a sum like that. Four goes into four?
Ryan:	*[pause]* One.
T:	Okay?
Ryan:	Yeah.

Ryan continues to work on his sheet in a desultory way, occasionally asking his teacher for help. At the end of the lesson the teacher tells the class that the activity was hard, and reassures them with 'don't worry if you got anything wrong'.

Reflections on the percentages lesson

This is a lesson of two main parts. The first part is in many ways typical of current mathematics teaching, with lots of interactive questioning at a high pace, involving the whole class. Margaret Sangster [Reading 2.3] considers some issues about pace which may be relevant here for Ryan. The second part is perhaps closer to the kind of lesson which parents might recall from their own schooldays, with individual differentiated work on exercises to practise the ideas raised in the first part. Ryan stays engaged for quite long periods, but there are times when he finds the work going too quickly for him or he cannot follow the more complex ideas, and he then becomes disengaged. His answers to several of the teacher's questions suggest his understanding of the lesson topic is somewhat limited.

What do children do if they need help during a mathematics lesson? Some of the parents we talked to remembered taking their books to the front and waiting in line for the teacher to help them. Nowadays children are more likely to remain seated and wait for the teacher to come to them, as Ryan's teacher does here. When she does arrive, it is not clear how helpful Ryan found her questions. They seemed to be aimed more at 'funnelling' Ryan towards giving the right answers than at engaging with him to help his basic understanding.

Nadia and the area lesson

At the start of the lesson Nadia is sitting on the carpet facing the front of the class. The rest of her classmates are either sitting on the carpet or on chairs at the back of the carpeted area. In front of them is a portable whiteboard on which the teacher will demonstrate the lesson.

The teacher introduces the session by saying it will be on 'area'. He asks children to describe what is meant by 'area'. The girl next to Nadia puts up her hand and answers, 'It's a place like Roath' (an area of Cardiff). The teacher explains that 'area' in mathematics is something different, and defines it as 'the amount of squares covered by anything'. He illustrates this by holding up a picture postcard. Looking at Nadia, he asks her 'Can you point to a small area on the card?' Nadia says 'The stamp'. The teacher explains to the class that the area on the postcard is measured in 'centimetres squared' and proceeds to draw a small square on the whiteboard to illustrate this. He asks the children to estimate the size of the square and take guesses. The teacher asks Nadia, who responds with 'one centimetre'.

The teacher then produces a sheet of paper which has squares on a grid and informs the class that it's an example where 'every sheet of paper in my box is printed in a factory and the squares are exactly one centimetre square'. He writes up '1 cm^2' and asks the class, 'What does the '^{2}' mean?' The children don't know, and he explains that it is because there are two measurements.

The lesson continues. The teacher measures a square on the whiteboard and asks the class to estimate the length of the square. Then he says, 'If I place the postcard on the grid, how many squares would I cover? Let's see who gets the closest'. Some children make estimates but the attention of other children seems to be wandering. The teacher now asks the class how they would actually work out the number of squares the postcard covers. Nadia is still looking at the board and has her hand raised for the first time. Nadia says she would 'times it . . . if it was like 23 top and 10 at the bottom, 23 times 10 is 230'. Another child suggests they 'measure it with a ruler'. The teacher replies 'We are always looking for the easiest way so if I counted every square it would be easy. So if I go back to Nadia who said count the first row [15], then we can count down [10 rows going down]. So what do we write to show we know the method?'. Nadia and James have their hands up and Nadia looks at James for his answer. Her hand remains raised as James explains and the teacher writes his answer on the board:

Area = 15 × 10 = 150.

The teacher asks the class 'What's missing?' A child replies '150 cm'. The teacher adds the 'cm', but says something else is missing. He adds '^{2}' to the number, so it reads '150 cm^2'.

The lesson moves into the next part. The teacher has sheets of white paper of different sizes, and the children have to choose a partner and a shape. Together, they will work out the area of the shape, but he emphasises that 'every person has to have an estimate first'. Nadia works with Stacey. Nadia looks back at the whiteboard to see how the work is done and she smiles as she starts the task.

Nadia and Stacey quickly complete the first two shapes and start on a third. Stacey measures the side of the shape and Nadia asks, 'Stacey, what is 25 times 25?' Stacey replies, '20 times 20, and then 5 times 5'. She is working this out on her fingers.

The teacher stops the lesson and says, 'Some children are not working properly, the noise level is too high, you're not concentrating'. He restates the approach he requires and tells the class that to work out the area, he wants them to follow the steps he has outlined on the board, namely:

Shape (A, B, C, etc.)
Estimate   =
Area of shape A   = X cm × Y cm ('must measure and *not* estimate')
                        = . . . cm^2

Nadia has written the sums but has not given the estimate. Only one boy in the class has set out the work in the way the teacher has requested. Nadia is finding estimation a little difficult and measures the paper again. She asks Stacey: 'How do you multiply? – I've forgotten'. Stacey reads out her measurements for shape K:

Stacey: 27.9.
T: Are you sure?
Stacey: 20.3.

Nadia is getting frustrated and says 'Look Stacey – measure again!' Nadia takes the lead and Stacey now verbalises her calculations.

The lesson is drawing to its close. The teacher asks 'Who has managed to do five shapes?' No one has completed five shapes. The maximum number completed is four, and these children are allowed to leave for lunch in the first instance. Nadia is one of the children allowed to leave first. The teacher is unable to cover all the tables and check their work in the time before lunch.

Reflections on the area lesson

The area lesson covers a different part of the mathematics curriculum – that of shape and space – compared with the previous two lessons. Nevertheless it illustrates some of the same features as these two lessons. These include the use of whole-class interactive discussion to introduce the topic, followed by work in smaller groups, the use of oral and mental methods, and the recognition that more than one method is acceptable (e.g. when the teacher says 'we are always looking for the easiest way'). At the same time, the lesson shares with other school mathematics lessons the characteristic of being somewhat disconnected from real-life purposes and motives. While the whole lesson is spent estimating and calculating areas, no explanation is given as to why one might want to do this in the world outside the classroom.

In interview, Nadia's teacher described how he had changed his practice to adopt the new methods. He said that he was now much more into a routine of 'using the carpet, trying to do something that will interact, you know, a little session at the beginning which is interactive with the children'. He also recalled how the methods he now taught were different from those which he himself had learned:

> We didn't really have this . . . mental maths approach. That's, you know, that's relatively new, isn't it? It was more learning methods for doing something with paper and pencil really. It was a lot more of that.

Saqib and the lines lesson

Saqib attends primary school in the same city as Olivia. His class contains a number of pupils who need special support for their learning, and so there are four adults present during this lesson – the class teacher, two Learning Support Assistants (LSAs) and an Ethnic Minority Achievement Service (EMAS) teacher. As a result, it feels as if there are several 'mini-lessons' going on around the room.

At the start of the lesson the class teacher has written on the whiteboard:

> We are learning to recognise perpendicular and parallel lines.

As the children come into the room she asks them to sit with their 'maths partners'. Saqib claims not to know who his partner is, but eventually sits with another boy. The teacher gives each pair of pupils a whiteboard and pen.

The teacher announces to the whole class that the lesson is 'similar to yesterday's mental maths'. She asks the children to close their eyes and visualise a rectangle – the previous day the shape had been a square. She asks them to visualise the mid-point of the rectangle by thinking about the mid-point of a shorter side. The pupils are then told to open their eyes and draw what they have visualised on their whiteboards. Saqib looks around the room at the other whiteboards but doesn't do any drawing himself.

The teacher sets up the next task – 'Talk with your partner and name two shapes'. There is some interaction between the teacher and individual children about their shapes – for example, symmetry is discussed. The teacher shows a pentagon on the OHP and asks the whole class for its name. One pupil says 'pentagon' and the teacher says 'it's a pentagon because it's got five sides'. Saqib shows some involvement with the lesson but also has a conversation with another boy about wrestling cards. Saqib says he can get him some tomorrow for 50p.

In the next part of the lesson the class teacher uses the OHP to show pupils more shapes and diagrams. Some children have to move their chairs so that they can see the screen, and this leads to some pupils being in an 'inner circle' nearer the front and others still at their tables who are less engaged in the work. The teacher tells the children they should be 'just listening' now and draws two parallel lines on the OHP, asking the pupils to explain what they are. She then asks pupils to look around the classroom and notice parallel lines. One pupil suggests 'on the board' while Saqib continues to negotiate the sale of wrestling cards to his neighbour.

The teacher says that the next word is 'perpendicular' and gives a hint what the answer should be – 'It's something to do with angles'. A pupil offers 'right angle'. The children are asked to find perpendicular lines around the room, and one of the LSAs attempts to get Saqib involved in the task.

The teacher gives out individual worksheets concerned with identifying perpendicular and parallel lines. Each of the four adults in the room works with a group of pupils. Saqib tries to answer the questions, asking his teacher 'Is that right?' It seems that having not paid attention in the plenary he is trying to get individual support in his group. However the teacher replies 'You weren't listening. Stay behind. I've explained once, I'm not going to waste time here, I'm going to spend time somewhere else'. Later she returns to Saqib's table and gives him a personal explanation of how to do the worksheet.

As the lesson draws to an end the teacher brings the whole class together again. She goes over the topic of parallel lines again and conducts a 'question and answer' session on shape. She presents an octagon on the OHP and asks 'How many parallel lines on a regular octagon?' The bell rings for the end of the lesson and the children return to their tables, then leave the classroom, table by table.

Reflections on the lines lesson

This lesson shows several features of the structure recommended by the National Numeracy Strategy – a whole-class introduction, differentiated group work, and a final plenary to review what has been achieved in the lesson. The lesson also shows several examples of mental and oral methods – such as the teacher's suggestion that the children visualise the mid-point of a rectangle. It also involves a good deal of interaction and discussion, and is conducted at a high pace. At the same time, Saqib's involvement in the lesson is only partial, with his attention being elsewhere – particularly during the whole-class sections of the lesson. Indeed he seems to have evolved a strategy of ignoring the whole-class explanations but asking for – and here eventually obtaining – individual attention at other times. It is possible that the presence of several other adults in the classroom encourages this strategy.

As with the other lessons we have seen, there is little in the lesson which connects the topic of parallel and perpendicular lines to the real-life world outside the classroom. Rather, the teacher attempts to make connections to the pupils' immediate environment by asking them to locate parallel and perpendicular lines inside the classroom. This may have made the topic more concrete for the children, but it did not appear to have made it more relevant.

In interview, Saqib's teacher said she felt that the National Numeracy Strategy limited her creativity as a teacher, although she accepted this might be partly due to her own limited confidence:

> I would like it to be a bit more creative and I don't feel that it does – I don't feel it does, you know – I think it's too, it's just too rigid. I feel like everything's too prescribed and it doesn't give us much room for, as I say . . . or maybe the room is there, it's just my confidence in taking, making these changes.

At the same time she recognised that there were occasions when she had decided to abandon the standard structure of the lesson and respond to what was happening with the children:

> It was like in numeracy the other day, when they were doing the puzzle. They didn't want to stop and have a plenary, they were all like 'no, I know what I'm doing', and I was like 'plenary, must do plenary'. And I did at the same time think 'Well why not, can't I just not . . .? No one's watching me, you know – it doesn't matter, at this mo . . . you know, right now'. So we did just get on with it, because they were just so into it.

Conclusions

The mathematics lessons experienced by Olivia, Ryan, Nadia and Saqib illustrate a number of features of current primary mathematics teaching in England and Wales (see Box 2.2). These features may be quite different from the mathematics lessons experienced by the children's parents when they were at school.

Box 2.2

Features of current primary mathematics lessons which might differ from parents' experiences

- The use of different types of classroom organisation – such as whole-class, small group and individual work – within the same lesson
- The fast pace of lessons
- The high levels of interaction between teachers and children
- The presence of several adults in the classroom
- The focus on mental and oral methods
- The acceptance of different methods for calculations
- The use of aids such as whiteboards.

These lessons also reveal characteristics of the way mathematics is taught in school, which may be very different from the way mathematics is experienced outside school. For example, there is little attempt in these lessons to make connections between mathematical ideas, such as fractions and percentages, and the situations in which these ideas might be used in the home or wider community. We will pursue this issue further in the next chapter, when we look at children's experiences of mathematics outside school.

Further reading

📖 Reading 2.1

This paper discusses the Leverhulme Numeracy Research Programme which explored the effects of the National Numeracy Strategy (NNS). Results suggested that there were small positive effects on achievement, but that in many schools the effects were negligible or even negative. The paper questions the wholly positive picture put forward by government of the effects of the NNS.

Brown, M., Askew, M., Millett, A. and Rhodes, V. (2003) 'The key role of educational research in the development and evaluation of the National Numeracy Strategy', *British Educational Research Journal*, 29(5): 655–667.

📖 Reading 2.2

In this paper, Chris Kyriacou reports on a systematic review of evidence on the effects of the introduction of daily mathematics lessons in England. A systematic review looks only at papers directly relevant to the research question and so is very targeted on a narrow range of studies. The findings question what is meant by whole-class interactive teaching and suggest that setting too swift a pace has especially negative consequences for the confidence of slower thinkers. It suggests that some of the gains in achievement seen might be due to closer alignment between what is taught and what is tested.

Kyriacou, C. (2005) 'The impact of daily mathematics lessons in England on pupil confidence and competence in early mathematics: a systematic review', *British Journal of Educational Studies*, 53(2): 168–186. A version is also available at: http://www.standards.dfes.gov.uk/research/themes/Mathematics/pupilperformance/?view=printerfriendly

📖 Reading 2.3

Margaret Sangster's research involved observing lessons and considering the impact of 'pace' on learners. She proposes the idea that appropriate pace allows learners time to engage and think – so that too fast a pace can be as ineffective as too slow. She notes that the 2007 Primary Framework still emphasises a notion of 'briskness' which may not support all learners.

Sangster, M. (2007) 'Reflecting on pace', *Mathematics Teaching Incorporating Micromaths*, 204: 34–36. Also available at: http://www.atm.org.uk/mt/archive/mt204files/ATM-MT204–34–36.pdf

Chapter 3

Mathematics at home

In this chapter we look at the mathematics that children are engaged in at home or in their wider communities. We describe some of the activities which Olivia, Ryan, Nadia, Saqib and their classmates take part in – outside of school – which involve mathematics in some way.

We start by looking at activities that arise through everyday household activities and playing games. Next, we look at activities which more closely resemble 'school mathematics'. We end the chapter by looking at ways in which parents help their children with mathematics at home, and at some of the different methods they bring to this process.

We look at these activities with two questions in mind:

1. What are the main similarities and differences between home and school mathematics?
2. What kind of knowledge about home mathematics might help teachers in supporting school mathematics?

Weighing the cat and other everyday household activities

Olivia's classmate Ellie made a home video, showing how she solved a real mathematical problem. Her family are going away on holiday for two weeks, and during this time their cat will be looked after by neighbours. Ellie has to work out how much cat food to leave them. The cat food is in the form of granules – and the daily amount depends on the weight of the cat. So, she needs to weigh her cat. She has placed the bathroom scales in front of the camera but the cat does not want to stay on the scales by itself. She tells the camera how she's going to solve the problem:

> I'm going to weigh my cat. First of all I'm going to stand on the scales and tell you my weight. Then I'm going to stand on the scales with the cat in my arms and take that weight and tell you. Then I'm going to take away the first weight I tell you from the second weight, and the weight left will be my cat's weight. From that I'll be able to work out how much cat food my cat is going to need.

> *[Stands on scales]* My weight is forty-six point . . . forty-six and a half kilograms. *[Stands on scales, holding cat]* My weight with the cat is fifty-three kilograms.

In the next scene Ellie is holding up a piece of card on which she has written:

My weight + cat   = 53 kg
My weight   = 46½ kg
_____
              6.5 kg
_____

Ellie explains what she has done:

> We weighed each other and my weight and the cat's weight came to fifty-three kilograms. My weight on my own came to forty-six and a half kilograms. If you take my weight, which is forty-six and a half kilograms, from my weight and the cat's weight, which is fifty-three kilograms, you get six point five kilograms, so that's how much my cat weighs.

Ellie goes over to the packet of cat food and reads off from a scale that says a cat weighing between five and seven kilograms can have between 45 and 55 grams of cat food a day. She takes a sheet of paper and calculates 50×14, as the family will be away for two weeks. After a false start, and some discussion with her mother about how to do it, she eventually gets a total of 700. Unfortunately she has confused grams and kilograms and announces that her cat will need 700 kilograms of cat food for the two-week holiday.

Weighing the cat is an example of an everyday household activity which involves mathematics. It is a particularly interesting example, as Ellie seems to be bringing in some ideas from school mathematics to help her solve the problem – such as the notion of 'weighing by difference' and the way she represents the subtraction problem in writing. In our research we found lots of examples of mathematics being used in everyday household activities. A common example was cooking, which can involve weighing quantities, using multiplication or division to amend a recipe, calculating the time needed for different parts of the process, and switching between different units of measurement. Planning a journey or holiday can involve consulting bus or train timetables, setting a budget, and working out the most cost-effective means of travel. Programming the DVD recorder can also involve mathematics, as the following conversation with Nadia's classmate Bryn makes clear:

Bryn: Well sometimes, we've got Sky Box Office, that's like when you can rent videos off TV, and I'm the only one that knows how to do it, and it involves some maths when you have to add up how much it's going to cost you, and stuff like that, and when you want to watch it, times and stuff, or what time you want to watch it, and stuff like that, and I do that sometimes.

Interviewer: So you're programming . . . you have to work out . . . ?

Bryn: You have to work out what time you want it, work out how long the film's going to be, and then how much you've got to pay for it. And grappling with the 24-hour clock.

One important feature of these activities is that the underlying purposes are an integral part of household life. Among other things, this means that it is important for all those involved that the mathematics is carried out correctly. If a mistake is made, then an unnecessarily large amount of cat food will be bought, or someone's favourite TV programme will not be recorded, or their dinner will be ruined. Yet despite the central role which mathematics plays in their successful completion, these activities have not been primarily set up for the teaching or learning of mathematics. In this respect, among others, they differ significantly from the school mathematics lessons described in Chapter 2.

Mathematics and money

One of the most frequent ways in which mathematics occurs in everyday activities outside school is in calculations involving money. All four of the children featured in Chapter 2 were regularly involved in activities that involved money.

Olivia's mother worked as the manager of a centre for adults with learning disabilities. The centre held frequent discos for fund-raising and Olivia regularly helped run the soft drinks bar. This involved checking the initial float, giving the correct change, and totalling everything up at the end. When asked to make a video showing some home mathematics, Olivia filmed herself counting the change from a recent disco. In the video she is seen filling bags with different denominations of coins, adding up what she has got, and entering the amount in her mother's bank book.

Ryan liked to go swimming at the leisure centre with his friends. His mother noted how he had recently worked out how much money he needed for such a trip:

> He knows how much I'm giving him, because if he goes to the baths, he needs £1 to get in, 50 pence for the locker and then £1 for sweets *[laughs]* although he gets his 50 pence back, so he knows he needs £2.50. So he's counted there. And he doesn't know he's doing it, obviously like.

Here Ryan's mother is making the important point that Ryan may be doing mathematics without being aware of it – and this 'lack of visibility' is a common feature of much home mathematics.

Nadia accompanied her mother on shopping trips because her mother's English was relatively modest. Nadia's role was to read out the prices on the goods in the shops, check what was bought against the shopping list, and make sure her mother received the correct change. Nadia also kept a careful written record of how much pocket money she received, and how much she was owed. Her father described how he used the weekly giving out of pocket money as an opportunity to test Nadia on her mathematics:

> She needs a pound every week. We give her one pound every Monday, so sometimes, I give her 20p, 22p, 29p and so 'what's left over?' So we say 'It's 60p left' and she says 'No dad, it's 70p'. So she knows how much is left, so we can't cheat her!

We saw in Chapter 2 how Saqib spent time in lessons negotiating the sale of wrestling cards. According to his mother, this reflected a wider interest in money and what could be bought with it. Saqib's father was a taxi driver, and both his parents encouraged him to pick up any coins dropped by accident in his father's taxi. Saqib's mother said he was very good at counting up the change into batches for giving to charities. She also reported how a few years previously, when the family returned to Pakistan for a while, Saqib was quick to understand the local currency and the current exchange rate – and he also spent time on this visit helping out in the family shop.

Parents often notice when their children have reached a particular stage in handling money, possibly because it is a sign of their growing independence. Olivia's classmate Molly had recently been on a family holiday to Portugal, and her mother described how Molly realised she had been given the wrong change when making purchases at an airport. She was pleased that Molly went back of her own accord to rectify the situation:

> And in fact we were at the airport on Sunday and she went and bought her and her brother a Slush Puppie, and instead of the lady giving her back one euro she only gave her 50 cents. And she was very confident to go back and tell her 'Oh you've given me the wrong change', which she would never have done, there's no way she would have done that before. She may have come back to me and said

[hesitant tone] 'Oh I think . . . ' but she sorted all that herself, which is nice that she's confident, especially, you know, we were in Portugal airport, so it wasn't even . . . so I was pleased that she is doing that now – she *is* working things out.

Mathematics and games

As well as playing a prominent role in real life, money also features in many of the games which children play at home. One of the best known of these is Monopoly. Olivia's classmate Connor made a video of himself playing Monopoly with his father, mother and younger brother, Dylan. The game is full of mathematics. The players take turns to throw two dice and add together the numbers shown on them; they move their counters the appropriate number of spaces around the board; they buy property and houses from the bank; they pay rent to other players, and receive bonuses or fines for passing 'Go' or from landing on 'Chance'. They also have to make more strategic financial decisions about, for example, whether to buy a particular property or whether to pay a fine to get out of jail.

Connor is clearly familiar with the game and is a competent player. At one point he is on a corner square and throws a double five. He says 'ten' and moves directly to the next corner without counting the intervening squares – he knows that each side of the board has ten squares. He also helps his younger brother with some of the mathematical demands of the game. On one occasion, Dylan lands on Marlborough Street and wants to buy it (for £180) but thinks he cannot because he no longer has any £100 notes. Connor points out that Dylan still has a £500 note and that if he used it he would get both the property and £320 change. A group of American researchers has looked at how children use and transform their mathematical knowledge as they play Monopoly [📖 Reading 3.1].

Monopoly is a game which has its origins in America in the 1930s. But other games we encountered have very different cultural origins. For example, Saqib's classmate Dhanu made a video of himself and his elder brother Mithun playing Carrom. This game is extremely popular on the Indian subcontinent and in other countries with a substantial south-Asian population. It is played on a plywood board, on which players take turns to flick a large coloured disk (the striker) against smaller black disks and white disks. The object is to sink disks of one's own colour into one of four pockets at each corner of the board. Points are scored for sinking more disks than one's opponent, and an additional five points can be scored if a special red disk (the queen) is also sunk. (See www.carromuk.co.uk for a full description and history of the game.)

In the video, Dhanu and Mithun – whose family are of Bengali origin – play several games of Carrom at a high pace. They are clearly experienced and skilful players, with a strong shared understanding of the game. They seem to play different variations of the game, including one in which the black disks score five points, the white disks score ten points, and the red disk scores fifty points. As well as the additions and subtractions involved in keeping score, there are also geometric calculations to be made about angles as the disks are flicked off the side of the board and off each other. In addition, the players need to think strategically about whether to sink their own disks or block their opponent's disks. At one point, for example, Dhanu decides to flick a black disk between Mithun's white disk and the nearest pocket. Unfortunately he miscalculates slightly, allowing his brother a clear passage to the pocket. 'Good try', says Mithun as he sinks the white disk.

Carrom and Monopoly are games with extensive cultural origins. But we also found children playing games which they seemed to have designed or developed themselves. Ryan was filmed by his mother playing outside on the street with his younger brother and some friends. The street is in a quiet housing estate and there is little traffic. The game, which the children called 'Kerbs', involves taking turns to throw a football from one side of the street to the other. The aim is to hit the opposing kerb as near to the edge as possible, and this counts as 20 points. A near miss means the thrower can get a second throw, this time taken from the middle of the street, and a successful throw here scores 10 points. The game proceeds at a high pace and is clearly a well-practised routine for Ryan and his friends.

Despite their different origins, Monopoly, Carrom and Kerbs have some important characteristics in common. They are all competitive games, in which two or more players compete with each other to score more points or obtain more 'money'. Being able to add, subtract and compare totals is fundamental to such games. At the same time, players do not play games like Monopoly because they want to practise or improve their mathematical knowledge and skills. Rather, such games provide an enjoyable way of passing time with family or friends.

The motivation for the activity is clearly one difference between games such as these and the school mathematics lessons described in Chapter 2. Another difference lies in the nature of error, how this is detected – and by whom. In the school lessons the teacher is the main mathematics expert who indicates to the pupils whether or not their calculations are correct. In games played outside school, the other players take on this role, and monitor each other's calculations. If someone adds up their score incorrectly, or takes too much change when buying a property in Monopoly, then this is quickly pointed out by the other players. If they feel the mistake has been made deliberately, accusations of cheating may result. There is thus a range of possible social interactions around error in out-of-school games which are unlikely to take place at school.

Mathematics and play

Children's role-play may also involve both mathematics and money. In the interview below, Nadia's classmate Chloe describes how she likes to play at selling houses and holidays. She explains that in her play she recreates some of the mathematics that adults would need to engage in if they were really selling houses or holidays:

Chloe:	Like I pretend to talk to people and I like say 'How much money do you want to spend?' and 'What's the total money you want to spend?', and they'll say like '300,000 – something like that', and then I have to try and find them a house, like how many rooms they want – if they want like a 3-bedroomed house I have to try and look in . . . pretend to look in books for a 3-bedroomed house. And if they . . . like if they find . . . if they want one in like, say, [local area where she lives], but then they want one in, say, Newport, I'll pretend to go . . . I'll go on like the laptop and I'll look and see what one's the best quality and they have to choose and something like that. Then I write it all down, like where they're moving and how much they really want to spend, and then how much it costs, and then they have to write me a cheque out, and then I'll pretend to fax the cheques off, and then I'll do other stuff.
Interviewer:	And holiday selling, you said that's a game you like to play as well?
Chloe:	Yeah. I've got like these holiday books, like brochures, and I look in them and these people ask me if they want a holiday and I'll just like look for holidays and they say where they want to go. If they want to go to Spain, I'll say 'What part?', and if they say 'I don't know', I'll go on and I'll say 'Would you like to go to . . . ?' . . . wherever.
Jason (Chloe's brother):	Alcudia.
Chloe:	Yeah, Alcudia. If they want to go there, like, I'll try and find the cheapest holiday for them and stuff like that.

Here, mathematics is involved in a way which is different from competitive games such as Monopoly. Chloe is not interacting with real customers, who might be quick to spot any mistake in her calculations. Nevertheless, it seems important for her that her play has a degree of realism about it, and she uses her mathematical knowledge and skill to obtain the best property deal or cheapest holiday for her imagined clients.

Mathematics is also involved in Olivia's play with her collection of 'Beanie Babies'. She knows the financial value of each member of her collection (at the time of our project she had 135) and describes how she sorts and counts them:

Interviewer: So how do you keep track of 135 Beanies?

Olivia: I write down their names and I just have . . . well, in my room it's kind of shelves but it has boxes and stuff, and they're in there. So I just name the boxes – Box 1, Box 2, Box 3 – and there's eighteen boxes and stuff, and I just say like one, two, three, four, five, six in a box and then just add them up all together and keep a total and just cross out the old total and put in the new total when I get a new one, and stuff.

So far in this chapter we have seen examples of mathematics embedded in everyday household activities, as well as in games and play. In Box 3.1 we provide the opportunity to reflect on the differences between this home use (and learning) of mathematics and the learning that takes place in school.

Box 3.1

Reflections on home and school mathematics

We have now seen several examples of children engaged in 'home mathematics'. Some were embedded in everyday household activities, while others took place during games and play. What do you think are the key similarities and differences between mathematics activities at home and at school? You might want to think about some or all of the following questions:

- What is the purpose of the activity? Why is it taking place?
- What do the participants think they are doing? Do they think they are doing mathematics, or doing something else?
- What role do other children – such as brothers, sisters and friends – play in these activities? Is it the same role as they play at school?
- How demanding is the mathematics involved? How does this compare with what the children are learning at school?
- What happens when a child makes a mistake in their mathematics? How do they find out? Is this the same or different from what happens in school?

'School mathematics at home'

As Box 3.1 indicates, the examples of home mathematics which we have looked at so far differ in a number of important ways from the mathematics of school. However, this is not yet the complete picture of home mathematics. In our project we found many examples of children doing mathematics at home which seemed much more similar to the mathematics they were doing in school. We call this kind of mathematics 'school mathematics at home'. Other researchers, such as Brian Street, Dave

Baker and Alison Tomlin, have referred to this as 'school-domain mathematics on the home site' [📖 Reading 3.2].

One common example of 'school mathematics at home' occurs when children are doing mathematics homework set by their teachers. Practice and reinforcement are quite common purposes for such homeworks. In the following example, Nadia's classmate Chloe describes how she has to learn her tables over the summer holidays in preparation for going into Year 6:

Chloe: 'Cos in Year 6 now, we have to learn . . . this summer holidays, we had to learn our times tables like our name. Like if we say 'What's your name?' and we say 'Chloe' – really quick, we have to learn the times tables like that. So if we say 'Seven times nine?' we have to go – whatever the answer is – really quickly.

Interviewer: So are there some of them that you've already managed that kind of quick?

Chloe: Err, most of them. I just need to learn my sixes and my nines . . . no, my eights. That's all now, 'cos they're the hardest. I can't remember . . . I can't remember the pattern in them. So tonight I'll probably go up to my bedroom . . . I'll have a bath, I'll go up to my bedroom and then I'll probably just sit at my desk and just do it until I know them.

Interviewer: So when you get back in Year 6 . . . ?

Chloe: I'll know them.

'School mathematics at home' takes several different forms in addition to homework set by the school. Some children in our project received extra mathematics tuition from private tutors, and were asked to carry out 'homework' set by their tutor. Several children were set mathematics problems or calculations by their parents or by their siblings. For example, Olivia described how when she and her mother were on a car journey together she would ask her mother for mathematics problems which she would then attempt to do in her head:

Interviewer: What kind of maths problems does your mum give you?

Olivia: Just addition, subtraction, division and multiplication really.

Interviewer: Can you give me an example of what she'll ask you to do?

Olivia: Erm, 235 add 315.

Interviewer: And do you work that out in your head?

Olivia: Yes, I work that out in my head. Unless she gives me something harder, one that's a bit challenging, I probably take it in different steps and use my fingers as well.

Interviewer: So would you have a paper and pencil in the car then – would you write it out?

Olivia: Erm, not normally, I just kind of have to remember!

Interviewer: How does she know if your answer is right?

Olivia: Normally my mum works it out and says whether it's right or not.

Interviewer: That must be tricky. Is she driving as well, while she's doing this?

Olivia: Sometimes.

Interviewer: [impressed] I see, driving while working out maths problems!

These kinds of mathematics problems were not confined to car journeys. Olivia's mother described how when she was just 'pottering around, I might say to her "Oh what's eight eights, you know, I've forgotten?", and she'll have the answer for me'. Sometimes these problems were set in the context of role play, when the children played at 'schools' with their siblings or friends, and were given mathematics problems by the 'teacher'. For example, the video made by Nadia's family shows her working through a sheet of mathematics problems drawn up by her older sister. Some of the parents had bought commercially available mathematics workbooks or software packages, and the children worked their way through these at home.

Parents helping with home mathematics

We have already seen some of the different ways in which parents help their children with mathematics at home. Olivia's mother, for example, gave her mathematics problems when driving in the car or when 'pottering around' at home. Nadia's father gave her 'trick' questions when handing over her weekly pocket money. Saqib's parents encouraged him to collect coins left in his father's taxi. In addition, most of the parents described how they supported their children when they were having difficulty with the mathematical aspects of an activity.

One area where parental help is most likely to be explicitly asked for is with mathematics homework. Some of the children pointed out that help with school work may be more readily available at home, because at school they have to share the teacher's attention with the rest of the class. As Chloe put it:

> My mum's good, though, because she helps me all the time, and my dad. But with school it's just . . . with school as well there's more children in my class and the teacher can't always just come straight to you. If I ask my mum she will just come straight to me and ask me.

However while parents may be more readily available at home, this does not mean that they always feel able to help. As we saw in the last chapter, many parents lack confidence in their own ability to help their children, and sometimes another family member is called upon to help specifically with mathematics. In Saqib's family, difficult mathematics problems were often referred to Saqib's aunt – who lived nearby – particularly when Saqib's father was out working. Nadia tended to ask her elder sister for help with mathematics homework, while Olivia often phoned up her grandmother or grandfather for advice.

Even when help is available, it is not always accepted in a straightforward way. Sometimes this is because the methods used by the children's parents to carry out mathematical procedures are different from the ones which the children are being taught in school. As a result, conflict may arise between parent and child.

A vivid example of this comes from Ryan's family. His mother wants to help him with his mathematics at home but is aware that the methods she was taught at school are different from the ones which Ryan is currently being taught. As we saw in Chapter 2, her attempts to help often end with the two of them 'at loggerheads'.

In the video which Ryan's mother made, he is inside the house doing his mathematics homework. At one point he says he 'just wants to play out' but his mother tells him he has got to do his homework first. But Ryan is finding his homework difficult. His mother offers to help but he pushes her away and says 'I do it a different way from you'. He is trying to complete a page of two-digit subtractions, laid out in columns. He makes a series of mistakes of the following form:

$$
\begin{array}{r}
4\,3 \\
-\,1\,5 \\
\hline
3\,2
\end{array}
$$

In other words, rather than subtract the '5' in the units column from the '3', he has taken the '3' from the '5'. His mother comes over to check what he has done:

Mother: I don't think that's right, that one there [points to the subtraction above]. You can't take five from . . .
Ryan: You have to take three away from five . . . four, three, two. You don't get it, do you?
Mother: If I was doing a take-away sum . . .
Ryan: [getting cross] It's the way I do it – we do it a different way.

Mother:	[tries to explain how she would do it] To be able to take five away from three, you have to put one unit off the four, and put it on the three, do you not?
Ryan:	No.
Mother:	You have to.
Ryan:	[in a plaintive voice] You don't, not at my school you don't.
Mother:	That's not your answer, thirty-two . . .

Ryan's mother eventually manages to persuade him to do the subtraction by taking 1 from the 4 and adding it to the 3, to make 13. Ryan rubs out all the work he has done so far and manages to complete the page correctly. Later however he has another disagreement with his mother about the methods he is using for subtraction, and the following interchange takes place:

Mother:	I don't get that at all.
Ryan:	[crossly] Talk to the teacher then!

See ▱ Reading 3.3 for more discussion of this example.

The fact that parents are using different methods from the ones that their children are being taught in school need not necessarily lead to such a dramatic breakdown in communication. An alternative and potentially more valuable response is to embrace the different methods and learn from them. This seemed to be happening in the home of Nadia's classmate Farah. Her mother was educated in Cardiff while her father was educated in Bangladesh, and they both learned different ways of doing mathematics. Here, Farah's mother gives an example of their different approaches by describing their different methods for doing division:

Mother:	It's like divisions, the long divisions, we does it the easy way, but he [Farah's father] is like showing her the hard way as well, how to do it quickly. So I think she's practising that as well.
Interviewer:	So how does he do division?
Mother:	Err, you know the short divisions, where you have to write . . . like we do it in our head and then write it at the top. But with him they like . . . they subtract and everything, like they're doing like a short division, they're doing a long one, so they're like subtracting and adding and all these kind of symbols, where we just use the times table to do the division.
Interviewer:	So you sort of put the numbers in and then take them away?
Mother:	Yeah take them away, there's like . . . it's quite different, I didn't understand the way he was doing it at first, but now the way he does it I think is much easier than the way we do it. It's like working out more, like we do in a rough book or something, rough it out and then write the answer down, but he's like doing everything in the one, like doing it in rough and plus doing the answer at the same time.

Farah's mother had been an EAL pupil who had had difficulty understanding what was said in her mathematics lessons at school. She described herself as 'not that very good with maths', and felt that she had learnt about mathematics by listening to her husband's explanations, just as her children were learning from them too:

Mother:	I think because the children, when they're sitting down to do it . . . [?because my husband's?] explaining them I get more into the . . . you know, doing the different ways that they're doing, learn different methods from it.
Interviewer:	So if you come across one of the bits that's something you haven't done . . .
Mother:	Yeah, I would ask my husband what is it, to explain it properly. And then when I ask him, I see Farah and my other one, they come by me and just stand and listen to what he say. So they try different things as well, the way he's doing it.

Counting on fingers

One of the methods which Farah's father showed her was how to count in threes on her fingers, using the creases of the finger joints – the 'strands' or 'lines' as her mother called them. Farah's mother explained the advantages of this way of counting:

> This is much more helpful than counting the fingers . . . because with the fingers you have to have an extra hand or a pair of hands, but with the lines you don't need extra hands, so she was quite good at that.

Several of the families in our project who had South Asian origins used this method of counting. Nadia, whose family also came from Bangladesh, made a video in which she solves a multiplication problem by counting in threes on her fingers. In an interview, however, Nadia's mother says that Nadia has misunderstood this form of counting, and that 'the real method is counting in fours'. This is where the finger tip, the creases of the finger joints and the finger base each represent one unit, so that one can count up to 20 on each hand. Nadia was asked about these different methods in a subsequent conversation:

Interviewer: The other way of adding is from your mum, counting in fours, isn't it? Do you use that?

Nadia: I do threes and fours, because you can do three and four. Ones are easy. Twos all you have to do is just double the number.

Interviewer: So it sounds as if you use a mix.

Nadia did not, however, use this family-taught method at school. She didn't know if her teacher was aware of the method, nor did she want to demonstrate it to him. In this respect at least, she wanted to keep a boundary between her home and school mathematics.

The example of strand counting shows that families may have ways of doing mathematics at home which are different from those used at school. It also shows that teachers may sometimes be unaware of these practices, particularly if they do not come from the same cultural background as the family. (See also Baker *et al.*, 2003.)

Box 3.2

What aspects of home life might teachers want to know more about?

The activities described in this chapter suggest that there is a wide range of activities and practices taking place at home which may be relevant to children learning mathematics in school. In what ways might it be helpful for teachers to know more about aspects of children's out-of-school lives, such as the following?

- Children's interests and hobbies
- Children's roles and responsibilities in the household
- Parents' feelings and attitudes towards mathematics
- The ways in which parents use mathematics in their daily lives
- The methods that parents use to perform mathematical calculations

Conclusions

This chapter has illustrated the breadth of activities involving mathematics which children are regularly engaged with outside of school. It shows how mathematics can be involved in everyday household activities, as well as in children's games and play. The chapter also describes some of the ways in which parents might be helping their children with mathematical activities such as homework, and the range of mathematical methods which they might bring to these activities.

Taken together, Chapters 2 and 3 suggest that there are important differences between home and school mathematics. They suggest that there are areas of children's out-of-school lives where teachers might want to know more, just as there are aspects of children's in-school lives where parents might want to know more. In the next two chapters we describe some of the activities we designed to encourage a greater sharing of knowledge between home and school.

Further reading

Reading 3.1

This group of researchers observed children of different ages playing Monopoly and analysed how they were using and transforming their mathematical knowledge. The cultural and social context of playing the game shaped the mathematics the children used.

Guberman, S., Rahm, J. and Menk, D. (1998) 'Transforming cultural practices: illustrations from children's game play', *Anthropology & Education Quarterly*, 29(4): 419–445.

Reading 3.2

Brian Street, Dave Baker and Alison Tomlin have produced an extensive analysis of what they term 'home and school numeracy practices'. They see numeracy as essentially a 'social practice' and look for similarities and differences between home and school, and between different homes, to provide explanations for why some children achieve less than others in school mathematics.

Street, B., Baker, D. and Tomlin, A. (2005) *Navigating Numeracies: Home/school numeracy practices*, Dordrecht: Springer.

Reading 3.3

Martin Hughes and Pamela Greenhough analyse this example further in a book chapter. The tensions and conflict between Ryan and his mother are explored and the difficulties that homework can present are discussed. The need for careful consideration of homework tasks and parents' roles in supporting their children is identified.

Hughes, M. and Greenhough, P. (2007) '"We do it a different way at my school!" Mathematics homework as a site for tension and conflict', in A. Watson and P. Winbourne (eds) *New Directions for Situated Cognition in Mathematics Education*, 129–152, New York: Springer.

Chapter 4

Mathematics activities that take school to home

In this chapter and the next we describe some practical activities for linking home and school mathematics learning – what we have termed *home–school knowledge exchange activities.* These activities were developed and implemented by teachers at the schools attended by the children we met in Chapters 2 and 3, with the support of the mathematics teacher-researcher on the project team. We present the activities as examples which other practitioners can use as they wish – trying them out as described here, amending them to suit their own particular circumstances, or using them as starting points for developing their own ideas. Along with our suggestions about what to do and advice about practical considerations, we have included accounts of how things worked in practice on our project and what sorts of responses the activities received from different participants. This will enable readers to assess for themselves how the activities might be used, adapted or developed.

Knowledge can be exchanged in two directions – *school-to-home* and *home-to-school.* At present, most information which passes between teachers and parents goes from school to home – what Jackie Marsh (2003) has called 'one-way traffic'. Much of this information is rather general. In this chapter, we describe some activities that we developed for communicating in this direction, which aimed to be more responsive to what parents actually wanted to know. We also incorporated methods, on occasion, that went beyond the use of the written word – which is usually the format for communication between school and home. In the next chapter, we describe activities where the flow of information is in the opposite direction, from home to school.

What do parents want to know about school mathematics?

A first step in developing school-to-home activities is to find out what parents actually want to know. Clearly there is little point in sending home information which parents already have or which they will not find useful. A good starting point might be to review existing forms of school-to-home information and try to obtain feedback on whether they are providing what parents want. Often this can be done through informal conversations with parents at the beginning and end of the school day, or through asking parents when they come into school at parents' evenings or other events. Alternatively, a small number of parents might be asked to canvas the opinions of other parents and feed these back to the school.

What our parents wanted

We used questionnaires (translated into home languages where appropriate) and parent discussion groups to find out more about what our parents wanted. They made several suggestions for improving school-to-home communication in general. These included:

continued

- Regular newsletters with information on what the children are doing each week in class
- More informal parent–teacher meetings and open days
- Surgeries to discuss concerns
- Fun activities that can be taken home from school
- Provision of interpreters at meetings.

In relation to mathematics, our parents wanted to know more about the National Curriculum, 'the big picture' as one parent called it. They wanted to know how mathematics was taught and detailed information on the methods being used, so that they could promote consistency between home and school when they tried to help their child. As one parent pointed out:

> I enjoy helping my child and would like to be more co-ordinated in my efforts. I am aware one of my sons needs extra help but I am often at a loss or concerned that I am confusing him.

They also wanted more information on their children's progress. Some parents made a number of specific suggestions as to how this kind of information might be conveyed. These included:

- Children taking home their school mathematics books regularly
- A home–school contact book
- Weekly/fortnightly suggestions of home activities that relate to the work in school (rather than a long list of suggestions of ways a parent can help a child generally)
- Workshops/handouts for parents, explaining approaches
- Relevant sections of the National Curriculum being photocopied and distributed to parents.

Parents also highlighted the need for information to be made available in home languages.

Activity 4.1 Parents visiting school (targeted invitations)

Inviting parents into school so that teachers can present aspects of the curriculum to them is not a new idea. However, teachers often complain that such meetings or workshops are poorly attended and that they do not attract the parents that the teacher would most like to meet with. One way of encouraging a better response is to target specific groups of parents and find ways of inviting them personally. Tailoring the meetings or workshops to the needs of the parents is also likely to improve the chances of parents engaging with the activity.

Parent visits to the classroom – what we did

In Olivia's class, the teachers invited a small group of parents, whose children were experiencing difficulty learning mathematics, to come into school and find out about the methods their children were using to carry out calculations. There were two teachers sharing the teaching of the class on a job-share basis. The teacher who was not taking the class on the day of the meeting offered to run the session for the parents. She showed the parents the ways the children might be expected to tackle basic operations and gave them reminder sheets to take home which illustrated the methods.

Parents may appear not to be interested in meetings about general topics, but they often respond better where activities are presented as being particularly relevant for their own child and as relating to their own concerns. Despite their interest, however, there may be many reasons why parents may find it difficult to attend on a particular occasion, including work commitments, child care or elder care. The constraints are likely to vary across parents. One of our parents, for example, lived some way from the school and did not have a car. She explained that meetings which abutted dropping-off and picking-up times for the children were best suited to her circumstances. It is clearly desirable if a variety of meeting times can be offered, including evenings. However, such arrangements can place a burden on school staff. One possibility may be to hold a meeting with a subgroup of parents who can then be prepared for cascading the content to others on a variety of occasions.

Our experience – what people said about classroom visits

Molly's mother was one of the parents who attended the methods-demonstration session. She was full of praise for the activity:

> They had an afternoon where some of the mums went in and they actually taught us for an hour how they teach children, and it helped so much. We got all these sheets and we came home and once I had it in my head – this is how she's got to do it. I mean the answer came out the same whether I did it my way or her way, but it was nice to know how they're being taught, how they break it all down. And she really did . . . even her teacher said they noticed such a huge difference, once I knew what she was doing and was able to give her more help . . . it was just breaking it all down and showing you how to do it. I mean she wouldn't have had a clue where to start, if you told her six times 350, but they show you how to break it down and she can do it really easily now, which is great . . . [It] was brilliant – probably the best hour I've spent at the school actually.

Olivia's mother was not one of those invited to the demonstration session because Olivia was achieving well in mathematics, but she had heard about it from others. She indicated that she would have had some reservations about such a session:

> I heard a group of parents had gone up for a maths lesson, and they were really scared and I thought 'Oh no'. Then they said 'But our kids are really struggling' and I thought 'Oh' but I was so relieved, 'Thank goodness they're not going to call me up there' . . . but I went away thinking 'Well actually that would be a really good opportunity.'

One factor in her trepidation was a concern as to how she would appear and compare to the other parents in the class:

> If they were struggling same as me it would be fun, but if they were far more able than me, that would really affect me quite badly.

We can see how this anxiety harks back to her school days, as we saw in Chapter 2, when she worried about saying her tables in front of others.

Where a small group of parents is singled out, care must be taken that the selection criteria are not presented in such a way that the children or the parents might be stigmatised by inclusion in the group. In our example, Molly's mother was delighted to be included as she felt the teachers were responding to her needs which had emerged during prior informal conversations about Molly's progress.

As we saw in Chapter 2, many parents have unhappy memories of school and their own mathematics learning. Being invited into school to sessions in which they feel they are going to be 'taught' can be daunting for some parents, especially if mathematics is involved, as we can see in the example of Olivia's mother. However, if those conducting the sessions are aware of these anxieties and fears, they will be more able to respond with sensitivity and to make arrangements that take account of such concerns.

Parents who speak English as an additional language (EAL) constitute another group where targeted invitations to sessions in school may prove effective. It is often the case that parents from these communities do not attend events in school, and where they do it is usually the fathers rather than the mothers. One way of making contact is for a member of the school staff to visit these mothers at home, accompanied by someone who speaks the home language and is able to translate.

Classroom visits for EAL parents – what we did

In Ryan's class, the Bangladeshi heritage parents were visited at home during the course of one afternoon by the teacher-researcher and a Bengali-speaking learning support assistant (LSA). They spoke with the mothers and explained that they were interested in the way the school could help parents participate more fully in their children's education. They invited them to a meeting with other mothers, the LSA and the EMAS (Ethnic Minority Achievement Service) teacher. Almost all the mothers who were visited attended the meeting – which was very lively. The parents discussed issues, before a spokesperson reported the outcomes of their discussions through the interpreter. The parents particularly wanted English and computer lessons to be set up at the school. The EMAS teacher recounted what happened:

> They wanted English lessons and they didn't want it anywhere but in the school. They understood that they could go to other places but they wanted to do it here, so we said 'Right, fine, we'll see what we can do'. And then they said they would like to know how to use computers because their children could use computers and they didn't know what they were doing – they couldn't even turn one on and off. So we said 'Right, fine, we'll see what we can do about that'.

These requests were subsequently taken up and implemented in the school. The parents were invited to join mathematics lessons and several responded to the offer, with mothers coming into school on the first Wednesday of every month. These lessons were ones in which the children supported by EMAS were taught separately. The mothers observed what was happening in the lessons and also made mathematics games for the children to play.

Figure 4.1 Mothers making games with their children

One decision that needs to be made about home visits is whether there will be any advance communication about the visit. A risk for the school where visits are unheralded is that parents might not be at home. Choosing the time of the visit carefully can help. In our case, the main function of the visits was to communicate about the forthcoming meeting so where parents were not at home, written invitations could still be used, although this was a less effective option. Parents may also be somewhat nonplussed by school staff turning up on their doorstep, particularly if they prefer to make a special effort to prepare the house for visitors and have refreshments ready. The visiting staff can however make it clear in a friendly manner that it is up to the family as to whether they are invited in. Our experience was that the parents were very welcoming. The alternative of attempting to organise mutually convenient appointments can be difficult and time-consuming, and can cause parents anxiety prior to the visit if they do not fully understand its nature or purpose. Normal common-sense precautions should be taken to protect staff making visits, such as visiting in pairs and carrying a mobile phone – and ID should be carried to reassure parents.

In respect to organising meetings for parents, it may be helpful with some communities if the school can arrange for meetings to be single-sex only. In an early interview, Rajinder's father observed that segregation of the sexes is common in many 'minority societies' with the implication that arrangements should attempt to take account of these sensibilities:

> It's awkward though, isn't it . . . one section for the men and one section for the women, really, because, it's like the minority societies are segregated anyway, and you'd have to cater for two types of parents, your males and females really.

In Ryan's class, the parents' interests were initially concerned with learning English and how to use computers rather than hearing about mathematics learning.

It is important to allow the parents time to express their own concerns and feel that these are being heard before moving on to the school's agenda – in our case promoting knowledge about mathematics learning.

Our experience – what people said about classroom visits for EAL parents

The parents were happy at being visited in their homes. Nandita's older sister-in-law translated for Nandita's mother as she spoke of the visit:

> She felt it was alright 'cos it's a mission for her to go to school and find out, whereas someone else came to her, it was OK . . . Because it was a same-language speaker, I think she was more open to ask questions . . . she liked the visit.

Over time, the parents who attended the mathematics lessons seemed to grow in confidence and feel more at ease in the school. The EMAS teacher observed:

> [At first] they met up in the yard beforehand and they came in en masse, now they come in on their own, and . . . walk upstairs, and they're not bothered if they're by themselves.

The children enjoyed having their mothers in the classroom, and their behaviour and standard of work improved when parents were present. This applied to all the children whether their parents were able to attend or not. The EMAS teacher said that the whole experience had been a 'real eye-opener' for her:

> Well it's been absolutely wonderful to have the parents coming in and working with the children, and you can't believe how pleased and proud the children are. They still . . . I mean they still get really thrilled when their mums come through the door.

It is somewhat unusual these days for children speaking English as an additional language to be withdrawn from their class and taught separately. In Ryan's school, however, this was the case for a proportion of lessons. When the mothers sat in on lessons, only the EAL children were present. It is possible that this grouping felt safer for the parents and may have created a relatively more comfortable environment in which their confidence was able to grow. It may be worth considering the artificial creation of similar small groups for EAL parents' initial visits to the classroom.

Activity 4.2 Making videos of mathematics lessons and activities

The focus of the previous section on targeted invitations and meetings was on face-to-face contact between school staff and parents. However, as we have already noted, parents may find it difficult to attend meetings or demonstration lessons because of work or family commitments. In this section we look at the use of video to communicate between school and home. The advantage of using video material is that it can be given or lent to parents who can then watch it at their own convenience.

From time to time, materials produced by the government or different agencies can prove useful. At the start of our project, a video entitled *Mathematics at Home and at School* was produced by the Numeracy Strategy with the support of the Basic

Skills Agency (now NIACE). It provided a summary of the principles behind the National Numeracy Strategy and the way mathematics was being taught in school, with suggestions of ways parents can support their children's learning at home. The video was free and a particular plus point was that it was available with voice-over translations in nine community languages. Our parents found it interesting and particularly mentioned the ideas for supporting mathematics at home as useful. However, it was very general, and whilst it indicated that children may use methods that are different from those of their parents it did not explain in any detail what those methods might be.

Making a customised classroom video focusing on what parents would actually like to know can be a more effective tool for communicating with parents. This approach has a number of advantages:

- A video allows individual schools and teachers to show parents how they specifically approach the teaching of mathematics.
- A video provides parents with a window on what is happening in the classroom which might otherwise be difficult to arrange.
- Making a video may be less disruptive than having groups of parents visiting a classroom.
- A school-made video that features their own child holds particular appeal for parents.
- Some parents may prefer to access information visually rather than through reading, while for some parents with limited literacy skills video may be the only means of communication.

Planning to make a mathematics lesson video

A key issue to address, when making a video in the classroom, is that of informed consent. While teachers do not need to obtain individual written permission from parents, they do need to inform parents in advance that their children will be filmed, and to give both parents and children the right to opt out if they want to. Parents also need to be informed about plans for the finished video – for example, who will receive copies and arrangements for screening.

The content of the video needs to be carefully planned by the teacher to decide what is to be filmed, why certain content will be included and how best to portray it. If practical, every child should feature in the video, and teachers also need to consider how far they will attempt to give equal time to individual children.

There are different ways the video can be shot and edited. Some teachers might prefer to have plenty of footage which can subsequently be edited down – and modern digital technology makes this a lot easier than it used to be. This approach gives more control over the content. Since the results will be made public, teachers may want to edit out some aspects – for example, if a child is being represented in a particularly poor light. However, it may be simpler to plan the content and timings in detail in advance, so that no further editing work is needed. It is also useful to set up a camera in the classroom prior to filming, so that the children become used to it and to the whole idea of being filmed. If teaching assistants are not featured, they can be asked to operate the camera.

It may be desirable to provide extra information along with the lesson content. This additional material might draw attention to or highlight particular features, provide explanations as to why certain aspects are the way they are or suggest ways that parents could build on or support what they are viewing. One way to provide such additional information is for the teacher to record inserts for the video. In these the teacher can explain what is going on and why things are happening in a particular way. It can be a little daunting to speak straight to a camera when producing the inserts. Teachers may find it more natural if someone asks them questions relevant to the lesson content which they then answer, speaking to the questioner rather than the camera.

Making videos of school mathematics – what we did

When we watched the videos of home mathematics made for us by a variety of families, we were impressed by the number of recordings in which the children acted as presenters and took responsibility for explaining what was happening (as in Ellie's account of weighing the cat in Chapter 3). We decided to build on these aptitudes and focused the school mathematics videos around groups of children demonstrating and explaining to camera the methods that were being used in their mathematical activities. This is in contrast to our literacy work, where edited versions of actual lessons were produced (see our companion volume *Improving Primary Literacy: Linking home and school*, 2007).

In Nadia's school, the children were shown in the video working in small groups, with one child in each group playing the teacher's role (explaining the procedures and asking questions) and the other children playing the role of pupils (answering the teacher's questions). They demonstrated different procedures relevant to their mathematical work, for example:

- Learning to multiply by 5, by first multiplying by 10 and then halving the answer.
- Learning to multiply by 50, by first multiplying by 100 and then halving the answer.

Some of the sequences were recorded in home languages, with Pakistani or Bangladeshi heritage children working together in groups to explain the same methods.

In Olivia's school, the video explored the use of systematic approaches to solve problems. The children explained the nature of a problem they had been given and then used a whiteboard to show how they investigated it. Olivia's group were investigating the ages of Jenny's three cats. They knew that the ages added up to 15 and that, when multiplied together, they made 45. Keeping the first cat at age one they systematically added a year to the second cat's age and decreased the third cat's age by one.

Cat 1	Cat 2	Cat 3	?
1	2	12	24
1	3	11	33
1	4	10	40
1	5	9	45

They kept a record on the whiteboard as they worked, and showed how they found an answer that satisfied the conditions.

Consideration needs to be given to how the video will be distributed or screened. Digital processing makes it relatively easy to create a copy for every family. However, the implications of making digitised pictures of children available outside of school need to be taken into account. Teachers may want to seek the agreement of parents that the materials will not be copied or posted on the internet. Producing a small number of copies in a read-only format, that families can borrow, watch and return, will increase control over the material but may result in more limited take-up on the part of parents, according to the degree of organisation involved in the borrowing arrangements. It may be possible to arrange a meeting at which the video is screened and the teacher is present. Such an arrangement will allow parents the opportunity to talk to the teacher about the content but may also reduce accessibility for some families. Providing a number of such screenings at different times of the day and in the evening will maximise the number of parents who are able to attend, but does make extra demands of teachers.

Our experience – what people said about the mathematics videos

The children enjoyed making the videos, although some said they had felt nervous at first. Bryn was one of the children tasked with 'teaching' a method to a group of 'pupils'. It transpired that he had created an additional agenda for his performance in the video:

> I tried to make it as fun as possible when I could, just to make him [the real teacher] see I made the people I was teaching laugh, and I thought that would show him that they enjoy it much more when they're allowed to laugh and have a little joke but do work as well, which he didn't get . . . but that's what I was trying to do – I was trying to show him how much better . . . how much more the kids would enjoy it if he made it funnier, and stuff like that.

The parents found the insights provided by the video helpful. Some of them also recognised the educational benefit for their children of an activity that encouraged children to produce explanations in their own words. Farah's mother commented:

> One time she had the chance to be a teacher on her own, so she had to think properly what to explain to the rest of the kids. She said she did find it difficult 'cos the way the teacher says it is really easy but when it comes to the children's turn she found it quite difficult, but she did get the hang of it . . . I did enjoy it 'cos it was like a whole new different thing they were doing, and it gave more chance for the children to speak out or have their own self-confidence in front of the video.

Farah was one of the children involved in producing a sequence in her home language. The task of expressing the technicalities of school mathematics in an additional language proved easier for some of the children than others. Farah confided:

> Another girl, she couldn't really speak properly in Bengali . . . I always have to tell her numbers and stuff like that . . . and in Bengali, she didn't know and I had to tell her, whisper to her.

Farah's mother pointed out that children's familiarity with a home language could be quite varied:

> 'Cos Farah lived in Bangladesh for five years and she'd been going to schools and all that, she's more experienced than the girl which was beside her.

However, she appreciated the inclusion of the sequence and was even teaching Farah and her sister more Bengali, 'so next time, if they do a video, she'll be explaining more properly in Bengali what words to use or what letters to use'.

continued

The parents of Olivia's class did not get a chance to see the video. The teacher felt that the explanations presented by the children in their groups were generally not clear enough to communicate methods to parents and decided not to use it.

> I did a bit of footage with them actually all working on different problems. They were all completely on task and talking about it and it was all really interesting, but then when they had to stand up and present that, it was a further level of thinking that they just couldn't do. They could explain it to me and say – look, we did this, this and this, and you know, not in necessarily clear mathematics vocabulary, but they were able to explain what they'd done. But to present that to video – that's another level of thinking. It's another higher order I think . . . you can glean from it what they did, but not in any way that could teach anybody else. I think parents would come away more confused than ever.

In this case, a straightforward record of a lesson – with the teacher explaining the methods used – might have been more successful.

Activity 4.3 Home–school jotters and files

The home–school jotter

One of the simplest means of communicating between school and home is to use a note-book that travels back and forth, in which messages can be written by school staff. If parents are also encouraged to write in the book, then it can act as a channel for communication in both directions.

The home–school jotter – what we did

In Olivia's class, a jotter was used as a contact vehicle between home and school. The children, as well as the adults, were allowed to write comments in the book, therefore allowing all parties to communicate. Connor's mother described its use:

> School has started a little notebook home system – I don't know whether you've seen it – where it's an opportunity for them to write in a note for us, but also for Connor to write in – or me to write in – and it goes back because . . . in case you can't get in to talk to them or something. And something recently happened and I noticed Connor wrote a bit about it. It was a bit of a spat with another boy, and he wrote it in this notebook and the teacher picked it up from there, although I don't think he would tell her . . . I don't think he would approach the teacher about something like that.

Our experience – what people said about the home–school jotter

Most parents were very enthusiastic about the jotter. Anthony's mother thought it was brilliant:

> They've started this jotter where if you've got any problems you can write it, which is brilliant . . , and because the teachers tell me, whereas before unless you made a point

continued

of going to see the teacher, then you wouldn't get to know about it, and there were lots of things that they told me . . . and also Anthony put his feelings down, because the front was for him and the back was for me, so he'd write things like 'So and so's annoying me when I'm doing my maths' or 'I can't concentrate' . . . or 'I don't like maths'. . . . It was nice that he could write his feelings down rather than taking them out on me or his brother.

Molly's mother also felt that it was very useful and appreciated the way the teachers got back to her on the points she raised. She felt it was important that it was an open system and that the adults' comments were not hidden from the child as, for example, in a letter in an envelope.

Olivia's mother felt the jotter was 'fantastic' since she did not get a chance to talk to the teachers before or after school because of her work. She recognised, however, that the written word (without the support of intonation) can be open to different interpretations and consequently to misinterpretation:

It can be very hard interpreting someone else's written word . . . because Mrs X had written 'Didn't you get one of the newsletters?' and I thought 'Oh, I'm being told off', but then I realised that, you know, I wasn't at all, and when I went back through the files I found the newsletter that had the information on there. That was quite amusing – but no, I think it's very useful.

Although the home–school jotter was popular, some families made less use of it than others. Some parents saw it as a way of getting in touch with the school when there were problems and consequently did not use it if there were no problems and everything seemed to be going fine. However, Suzanne's mother commented that if there were a problem she would prefer to actually speak to the teacher. Connor's father suggested that more use could be made of email as an informal channel of communication.

A home–school notebook is more likely to meet with success if all parties feel that its use chimes with their own purposes and feel relaxed about writing in it. Clearly, an important limitation on its use relates to the capacity of parents to engage with written text. Reading communications from the teacher may prove a particular challenge for families where English is an additional language. It may help if language support staff are able to provide written translations into home languages. However, parents may not be literate in their native language. Leena's mother, for example, was not fully able to read Somali and preferred to receive information in English, which Leena's sister then translated. Where schools are considering providing large amounts of written material in home languages, it would be worthwhile finding out from parents how desirable this might be.

The home–school file

Using a notebook or a jotter requires the teacher to make entries by hand, one by one, across a set of books. This is a strength, in that comments are tailored to the individual child, but this approach can be very demanding in terms of a teacher's time. It is more economical if the teacher is able to duplicate copies of some of the texts where they are appropriate for groups of children or the whole class. However, individual pieces of paper are easily lost or left at the bottom of a bag. Using a home–school file or folder rather than a book provides more flexibility, allowing duplicated sheets to be incorporated in the set of communications sent home. At the same time it provides a storage space that is unlikely to be overlooked and can promote continuity if pages are kept over time.

A dedicated file for school-to-home communication about mathematics could contain a variety of sections. Based on the sorts of information our parents mentioned, it might include:

- General information about the curriculum in general, possibly utilising government publications
- Information about a particular topic that children will be working on
- Objectives or targets related to the topic
- Explanations of key words or ideas
- Information about the activities that will be used in school
- Ideas as to how to provide help
- Suggestions for activities to carry out at home
- A commenting space or system
- Information as to how a particular child is getting on, difficulties, successes
- Guidance about specific areas that would benefit from more attention
- Information about additional resources, e.g. useful websites
- Games to make and play that are relevant to a topic.

The home–school file – what we did

The children were given an A5 ring binder with their laminated photograph and name on the front. This personalisation was designed to encourage the children to look after them. A letter explaining the use of the home–school file was included on its first use. The teachers sent home a variety of materials in the folders, including copies of publications like the BEAM pamphlet for parents 'Mathematics learning in Year 5'. They also included games that the family could make and play, and activities to carry out, with parental help. Resource sheet 1 (see over) shows an example of such an activity, investigating the age of a car using its number plate.

For the last part of the activity in that 'real-life' investigaton, one boy suggested the dimensions for the garage as 'length 5m 46cm, hight 2m 55cm and width 2m 57cm'. In the Any comments? space, his father had written 'Without any help from me (a builder) Jay has designed almost exactly a standard single garage. Well done. Dad'.

Sheet 2 shows an example of where a number of aspects have been brought together on one page.

It is important that parents know what is expected of them in terms of the content of a home–school file. This is particularly the case where different types of material are included. Some sections may be for information only and require no action other than reading. Other sections may contain rather general suggestions for action – things that can be borne in mind as parent and child interact – while others may be suggestions for activities where parent and child both get involved, sitting down together to carry something out. It may help if the type of action required is spelled out. It also helps if communications can be made as specific as possible – for example, supplementing information about the content of an upcoming topic with details about the period of time it will be a focus for learning. Furthermore, different kinds of material will imply different expectations as to how often the file travels between school and home and how often the parent might be expected to look at it. Here again it is helpful if expectations can be made clear.

Sheet 1

School

Date

Topic: real-life investigations

Did you know that you can tell the age of a vehicle by its number plate?

Before September 2001, the age of most cars was shown by the single letter at the beginning or end of the number plate.

Look for these letters by themselves at the start of a number.

K = 1992/93	S = 1998/99
L = 1993/94	T = 1999
M = 1994/95	V = 1999/2000
N = 1995/96	W = 2000
P = 1996/97	X = 2000/2001
R = 1997/98	Y = 2001

Since September 2001 new number plates are usually made up of 7 characters (5 letters and 2 numbers). The 2 numbers show the age :-

01 means registered between Mar and Aug 2001
51 means registered between Sep and Feb 2001/2002
02 means registered between Mar and Aug 2002
52 means registered between Sep and Feb 2002/2003
03 means registered between Mar and Aug 2003
53 means registered between Sep and Feb 2003/2004

Some tasks:

- Work out the age of a car that belongs to someone you know, by looking at the number plate.

- If the average car travels 8,000 miles a year, is this car low, high or average for its age?

- *Estimate* the wheel circumference in centimetres and *then* measure it. (A piece of string might be useful here.)

  How many times does the wheel make a complete turn when travelling 100 metres?

- Measure the length, width and height of your car. Suggest dimensions for a garage.

Any comments?

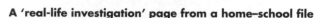

A 'real-life investigation' page from a home–school file

From: Jan Winter, Jane Andrews, Pamela Greenhough, Martin Hughes, Leida Salway and Wan Ching Yee, *Improving Primary Mathematics*, London, Routledge © 2009

Sheet 2

School	Class

Topic: decimal numbers	Date

Key words: metre, centimetre, tenths, hundredths, decimal number, decimal point.

Objectives: To know that the decimal point separates the whole numbers and the parts of numbers.
To know that the number to the left of the decimal point is the units (whole numbers) and the digits to the right are tenths, then hundredths.
To know that when ordering decimal numbers, to look at the number of units (wholes) first, then tenths, then hundredths.

Class activities:
- Using metres, as a unit of measure, order decimal numbers, e.g. 3.4m, 3.04m and 4.3m according to size.
- Using a number line, locating the position of decimal numbers.
- Using place value cards to order decimal numbers.
- Recognising the value of decimal numbers to the nearest whole number.

Home activities:

Let your child measure objects around the house using a measuring tape marked in metres and centimetres. Help them to remember that 1 metre 25 centimetres can be written as 1.25m. Using decimal notation ask them to write down the measurement of objects longer than 1 metre and then by just using the decimal numbers order them according to size, either the longest first or starting with the shortest.

If your child has any difficulties understanding decimal notation then let the teacher know by writing down your concerns in the Comment box below.

Parent / teacher comments:
(This space is for both parents and teachers to comment on the topic or the activities related to them. Please feel free to ask any questions or make any comments)

A topic-based page from a home–school file
From: Jan Winter, Jane Andrews, Pamela Greenhough, Martin Hughes, Leida Salway and Wan Ching Yee, *Improving Primary Mathematics*, London, Routledge © 2009

Where ideas for activities are included in a file, there may be questions as to the ways in which they relate to homework. There can be overlaps, and many of the issues relating to homework may need to be considered in relation to the home–school activities. For example, if the intention is for parents to help with an activity then a significant amount of time may need to be given for completion so that the activity can be inserted into busy timetables. Parents may feel that activities are only valued if they are returned to the teacher and the teacher's feedback obtained. This can result in a push towards activities in which there is some record or concrete product involved that can be taken back to school. Using games can counter this impulse. A further question concerns whether the activities should be differentiated according to the child's ability – and how this might be achieved. (The interested reader can find more detailed information on parents', children's and teachers' views about homework, and on homework practices in our reports from a previous study, see Hughes and Greenhough 2003a and 2003b.)

Our experience – what people said about the home–school file

The parents particularly liked the games that were sent home. Gavin's mother recounted how Gavin's younger brother had got involved as well:

> There were some game things in there he had to work out. I know it confused me at one point where you had to join some things up and that . . . and, ooh, there was puzzles and all sorts in there, wasn't there, but we did actually enjoy it all together. The three of us tried to figure it out – it was good.

Some parents were unsure of their role in relation to the folder. Things only became clear for Farah's mother after she had talked with the teacher:

> At first I didn't understand what to do with the folder, 'cos she's been bringing some sheets and I thought that you just read it and then you just put it in the folder . . . but then when I had a word with Mr X he said that when she takes the sheet home that means that they're doing some of the work in school, they use that kind of method in school, so . . . and you have to put comments, and all that.

Olivia's teacher was determined to make the activities relevant to both school and home, and she tried to incorporate children's ideas in the activities she designed rather than using 'off the shelf' materials. This was very time-consuming and meant that she was unable to send things home as often as she would have liked:

> [I tried] to link the objectives that we were covering in maths in class with opportunities to work with their parents at home. So, to make the parents aware of what we were doing and to try and link it to something real . . . I think they were successful but I just couldn't sustain the work. . . . It wasn't something . . . well I didn't feel it was something that . . . because I wanted it to be personal, I just couldn't get a resource that had already been made. . . . And it wasn't something I could prepare in advance either, because we'd maybe been talking about something in maths and saying 'Well, practically, where does that fit in our everyday life?' or 'Can you think of examples where you might use this?' And they'd say something and I'd use that idea. . . . But it got good responses from the parents and it was interesting to read what they'd done. . . . Parents were saying this is exciting and interesting and the children were coming back with that feeling – 'Oh yes this is an interesting thing to do'.

Conclusions

This chapter has described our experiences of activities that promoted the flow of information from school to home. The success of the activities is indicated by the comments we quote from parents involved. The range of schools we were working with was varied, so different strategies had success in different schools. In some cases the activities provided a new way for parents and children to interact mathematically as well as providing communication between school and home.

Box 4.1

Reflections on school-to-home knowledge exchange

- How might teachers share the mathematical methods that children are learning in school?
- How might teachers support parents who are not confident in their own mathematical skills?
- How might teachers support parents who do not speak English at home with their children?
- What kind of activities could help parents and children enjoy mathematics at home together as well as supporting learning?
- Is there a danger that some activities could reinforce parents' negative feelings about mathematics? How can this be avoided?

Chapter 5

Mathematics activities that bring home into school

In this chapter we continue looking at practical activities which link home and school mathematics learning. Here, our focus is on activities that bring aspects of the home into school. As in Chapter 4, we present these activities as examples which other practitioners can use as they wish – either trying them out as described here, amending them to suit their own particular circumstances, or using them as starting points for thinking about new activities.

One area in which knowledge of the child in out-of-school settings is seen as increasingly relevant is in the context of assessment. Traditionally, this has been at its strongest in the Early Years. The potential contribution of parents is highlighted, for example, in the *Statutory Framework for the Early Years Foundation Stage* (DCFS, 2008) where it is suggested that all adults, including parents, who interact with the child should contribute to the assessment process. Practitioners may wish to consider what types of information from parents they would find most useful. They might also think about what types of information parents might want to share with them.

What our parents wanted to share with school

In general, our parents admired how well the teachers knew their children and appreciated the efforts the teachers made to understand them. However, they felt that large class sizes made it difficult to know every child in depth, and they recognised that teachers only saw children in a restricted range of contexts. On the whole, they felt that teachers did not make full use of parents' knowledge of their children.

The parents attending the discussion groups were asked what information or knowledge about home or their child they wanted to give to school or the teacher. They suggested the following:

- Things the child enjoys or dislikes doing at home
- The child's interests
- The way the child approaches home tasks
- The child's preferred methods of learning (e.g. from a book or from a computer and the internet)
- Home events that might be affecting the child
- Worries a child might have.

Most of this information related to the child at home. However, parents also mentioned aspects of school life where they might have a perspective that was complementary to that of the teacher. For example, one mother mentioned that her child loved football and was very disappointed not to be picked at school. She thought the teacher was unaware of his interest or his feelings.

Our parents suggested questionnaires or profiles with tick boxes as ways of sharing information. The following photocopiable resource sheets show a form that might be used as a start in creating a child's out-of-school profile.

continued on p. 47

Pupil Profile Sheet 1

Pupil Profile

School: **Date:**

Full name:

Name liked to be called:

Address:

Date and place of birth: :   :   /

Names and ages of brothers/sisters:

Languages spoken (other than English):

Any other information you would like the teacher to know about your family:

Pupil's attitude towards mathematics (Do they enjoy it? Find it easy or difficult? Worry about it?):

Any other information you would like the teacher to know about the pupil:

From: Jan Winter, Jane Andrews, Pamela Greenhough, Martin Hughes, Leida Salway and Wan Ching Yee, *Improving Primary Mathematics*, London, Routledge © 2009

Pupil Profile Sheet 2

Hobbies and interests: what do you do in your free time (when not at school)?			
Activities	Sometimes	Often	Never
Watch TV or videos			
Play computer games on your own			
Play computer games with someone			
Play other indoor games (not electronic)			
Play with toys (figures, cars or dolls)			
Draw or colour pictures			
Read books			
Write stories/letters			
Play outdoors (on skates, skateboard, bike or scooter)			
Play outdoor games			
Go to a leisure centre			

What clubs do you belong to?

What new skills are you learning?

What is your favourite out-of-school activity?

What else do you do in your free time?

What is your favourite subject in school?

Do you like mathematics?

From: Jan Winter, Jane Andrews, Pamela Greenhough, Martin Hughes, Leida Salway and Wan Ching Yee, *Improving Primary Mathematics*, London, Routledge © 2009

The first page was designed for parents to complete, giving them the opportunity to share any information about their child or family that they felt was important for the teacher to know. The questions about the family were left somewhat vague so as not to appear intrusive. The respect for family privacy was emphasised in the letter that accompanied the form. The second page was designed to be completed by the parent and pupil together.

How might parents share their knowledge with teachers? In some schools it might be possible to do this through informal conversations at the beginning and end of the school day. This is easier in some schools than others. Sustaining a teacher–parent dialogue is much more difficult when children are picked up from a busy playground or attend an after-school club. In contrast, when parents are able to collect their children directly from the classroom it is easier to maintain relaxed, two-way conversations. However, we should also recognise that parents are less likely to collect their children from the classroom as they get older.

Some of the information that teachers and parents want to share might not be forthcoming in informal conversations but would be better addressed at a dedicated meeting. Arranging and attending this sort of meeting can make demands on parents and teachers alike, and alternative methods for developing an exchange of information might suit some schools. For example, a brief questionnaire might be sent home at the beginning of each school term or year, which parents and children could fill in together (see the Pupil Profile photocopiable sheets for example). In some schools, setting aside an extra five minutes during a parents' evening might work better than sending home a written questionnaire.

However, knowledge-sharing in the home-to-school direction can involve more than the kinds of information suggested above. It is important that home knowledge should be built upon and brought into the learning that children do in school. In Chapter 3, we saw some of the varied ways children were developing understanding of mathematics in their out-of-school encounters. It is desirable that knowledge exchange in the home-to-school direction should also try and find ways to bring children's own out-of-school knowledge into school. Inevitably this means that the children as well as the adults will be involved in linking the two worlds of home and school. In the rest of this chapter, we look at activities designed to support this kind of exchange.

Activity 5.1 Taking photographs of everyday maths

As we saw in Chapter 3, children engage in a wide range of mathematical activities at home. Photographs can be an effective way of sharing information with teachers about these activities and can provide a richness and immediacy which children may find hard to communicate in other ways. They can help children make connections between their home and school mathematics. Furthermore, the decisions involved in taking photographs often involve children in creating and formulating mathematical problems rather than looking for solutions to problems posed by unknown others. The experience of looking for embedded mathematics and formulating problems adds a further dimension to children's mathematical understanding.

Everyday maths photographs – what we did

Disposable cameras were given to all the children in our project and they were asked to take photographs of any mathematical activities they took part in over the summer holiday. They were also given a diary-type booklet in which to write down when they took each photograph and who was involved in the activity with them, as well as a very brief comment about what was taking place. Before the booklets and cameras were distributed, teachers discussed with the children what was meant by 'everyday maths', and children were asked to make suggestions about the sort of activities that might take place. It was emphasised that everyday mathematical activities were what was required, rather than the usual school-type mathematical activities, which took place at home. It was decided that working from a published workbook was not to be included as an everyday maths activity, nor was working with a parent, family member or tutor on 'school-type' written calculations. Suggestions were given in the booklet for possible everyday mathematical activities and the children were encouraged to add their own, in discussion with their parents. (See the examples of everyday mathematics page from the following photocopiable sheets for sample pages from the booklet.)

The cameras were returned to school after the holidays to be developed and the photographs were returned to the children, who selected the ones they wanted to share with the other children in the class. The photos covered a wide range of everyday mathematics activities. For example, Nadia's classmate Bryn took a photo of a water pistol that had to be pumped up to a particular pressure before it could be fired. As he told us later:

> My mum bought me a present, I can't remember what it was now. . . . I think it was just like a . . . oh I know, it was like this water pistol with a rocket, you pump it, that's quite good actually. It's got numbers on it and you've got to pump up so the water comes – it's upstairs – you've got to pump up and the water comes up, and when it gets to a certain number you've got to pull it back and it goes flying into the air with water spraying behind it.

Olivia took photographs of train and bus timetables and her mother described the mathematics involved:

> We actually caught the train and then the bus and she worked out the timings and the mileage, so it was a really good thing for her to do.

Olivia also photographed weight and height restrictions on a road and checked that their car was within the restrictions:

> I took photos of the, erm . . . you know, on the road, how heavy a car can be or something, took photos of that and looked in the manual and stuff to make sure it was all right and stuff.

The selected photographs were subsequently used in two slightly different ways. In three schools they were used to make a class album, while in one school they were used to create a large display. To make the class album, each child selected two photographs and wrote a brief explanation of the mathematical activity that the photograph represented. (It could be difficult to read the mathematics directly from the picture. For example, a photo of a pair of trainers could represent the calculation as to the number of weeks of saving involved before they could be bought. Another child took a photo of a family photograph of his grandparents' wedding day, another of his grandparents now and calculated how long they had been married.) Figures 5.1 and 5.2 (on pp. 53–4) show examples of the photographs.

The photos and writing were mounted on A4 pages which were assembled into an album. This was then made available for other pupils and teachers to read, and also parents when

continued on p. 55

Everyday Mathemathics Sheet 1

Everyday mathematics

What is everyday mathematics? We all, children and adults, do mathematical calculations every day. For example, every time we look at a clock and work out how long we have got before we have to go somewhere or do something, we are making a mathematical calculation.

At the back of this booklet there is a list of activities you may be involved in where you carry out mathematical calculations. Can you add some of your own?

What we would like you to do is to jot down in this booklet, any occasion when you think you have carried out some everyday maths, and whether you did it alone or who else was involved.

A camera has been supplied for a photograph of some of these events to be taken.

When you return to school, please return this completed booklet and the camera and we will get your photographs developed. (If you wish to have the photographs developed yourselves and bring those back to school, that is fine.)

Your photographs and booklets will be the starting point for discussions about everyday maths with you, your parents and your teachers.

Don't worry if you do not fill the booklet or use up all the film – just do as much as you can. You may want to take it on holiday with you or on a day out, just to show that we do maths even when we are enjoying ourselves!

From: Jan Winter, Jane Andrews, Pamela Greenhough, Martin Hughes, Leida Salway and Wan Ching Yee, *Improving Primary Mathematics*, London, Routledge © 2009

continued

Everyday Mathemathics Sheet 2

Examples of everyday mathematics

1 Looking at a clock and telling the time; working out how long it will be before you have your tea, or go out or watch your favourite programme.

2 Looking at a timetable (bus, train, flights, etc.) and working out what time you need to arrive at the station, airport, etc. to catch that bus, train or plane.

3 Using a recipe in a cookbook and weighing out ingredients or working out how much of each ingredient you need to buy.

4 When you go shopping, working out how much you will have to pay for a number of things – and how much change you should get back.

5 Playing any games (cards, darts, billiards, board games), where you have to work out the score in order to find out who has won.

6 Any activity that involves measuring, using a ruler or a tape measure.

7

8

9

10

continued

From: Jan Winter, Jane Andrews, Pamela Greenhough, Martin Hughes, Leida Salway and Wan Ching Yee, *Improving Primary Mathematics*, London, Routledge © 2009

Everyday Mathemathics Sheet 3

Date (and the day and time)	Activity (What you did)	People (Who you did it with)	Duration (How long it took)
Saturday 20th July 10 o'clock	Went to town on the bus and worked out from the timetable, how long we would be on the bus.	My mum and my sister	5 minutes

continued

From: Jan Winter, Jane Andrews, Pamela Greenhough, Martin Hughes, Leida Salway and Wan Ching Yee, *Improving Primary Mathematics*, London, Routledge © 2009

Everyday Mathemathics Sheet 4

Date (and the day and time)	Activity (What you did)	People (Who you did it with)	Duration (How long it took)

From: Jan Winter, Jane Andrews, Pamela Greenhough, Martin Hughes, Leida Salway and Wan Ching Yee, *Improving Primary Mathematics*, London, Routledge © 2009

Here is a picture of me playing Scrabble
I am try to make a letter with Seven words
each letter is worth a number. I am trying
to get a high Score by putting the letters on
the board. Some Squares are triple letter where
you have to times the number of the letter by
three. Some Squares are double word Scores
where you add up all the letter numbers in
the word and timesing the answer by two.

Figure 5.1 Playing Scrabble

I took a picture of my new trainers
because I went to town and saw the ones
I wanted but I didn't have enough
money because the cost £18 and I only
had £7. So I worked out how much money
I needed and I saved up the money and
bought them.

Figure 5.2 Saving for new trainers

they attended the school's open evening. It also formed the starting point for discussion on the wide range of mathematical activities that take place out of school. The photographs that were used for the display also had brief written explanations to accompany them, but the discussion took place whilst the children all shared each other's photographs before selecting some for the display.

We have highlighted the ways in which the awareness involved in taking the photos relates to the creation and construction of mathematical problems as much as their solution. One teacher, recognising this feature, came up with the idea of students working together in pairs to pose authentic problems for each other based on their own and their partner's photographs.

The photos could be sorted into sets to create resources relating to particular topics, such as money, weight and time. Using a more focused approach, the connection between everyday activities and a particular topic could be explored by specifically asking children to take photographs related to a particular topic prior to starting work on that theme.

Providing an individual disposable camera for each child in a class is clearly an expensive option. However, as the teachers pointed out, there are ways to adapt the activity to make it more affordable. For example, instead of every child being given their own camera a small number could be purchased for the class. The teacher could then organise the activity so that children shared the cameras and took turns to take three or four pictures each. Another option would be to use digital cameras on a rota basis – pictures could be downloaded on the class computer and would provide a valuable resource for future work. In addition, parents and children are increasingly likely to have mobile phones with cameras, and so photographs can easily be taken out of school and subsequently downloaded in school.

Our experience – what people said about the everyday maths photographs

Many children and parents enjoyed the activity. Nadia's father said:

> Oh yes, she was very happy and we were very happy as well. It's something different.

Some of the children tackled the task independently and relished having their own camera. Nadia's father remembered:

> She said 'The teacher gave the camera to me, you know,' so she said 'I'm going to take pictures and I'm not going to lend it to anyone'.

Sometimes, different members of the family got involved. Ryan's mother took several of the photos while Ryan did the mathematics:

Ryan: Remember that day we had to . . . if you do any sort of maths – like if I give the woman a tenner and then what change I'd get back – we had to [take a photo of it] with the camera.

Mother: Oh yeah, you were actually doing maths . . . if you were going to an ice-cream van or something.

Ryan: Yeah, if you've got . . . yeah, I'd give money then I'd count up the change.

Often family members helped with suggestions as to what the subject matter might be. Saqib's classmate Leena was helped by her older sister to think of some extra ideas:

continued

She ran out of ideas of things to take, but then she quickly learnt that they were everywhere. She said to me 'I've got twelve pictures left and I don't know what to take it of', so I was helping her out, saying 'It's everywhere you can see ideas'.

The activity helped children and family members recognise the mathematics inherent in everyday activities. Anthony's mother observed:

[It was] fun, I would say. He enjoyed doing it. And it also made him think about what we actually do in the house that involves numbers. Like the clock and telling the time, and going to the shops, and change, and money. Because that's another thing, him and [his brother] were changing their English money into euros, so that was more maths trying to work out that. And also trying to work out when we were on holidays, if something was eight euros how much was that in English money.

Molly thought the activity was a good idea 'because then they [the grown-ups] know that you are doing maths and learning'. Olivia said that she 'learnt that there's lots of different ways of maths, even though you can't see it that much'.

However, there was also recognition that the activity was challenging. Anthony's mother recalled:

A fortnight went by and we hadn't taken any pictures and I was thinking, 'Oh my god, what are we going to take pictures of him doing?', because he wasn't getting any maths homework. . . . And I was thinking, 'Well what do other people do?' – that was the other thing, I was trying to think of what other people did in their houses that involved numbers that I didn't do. I was thinking, 'I must be missing something here!'

Some children failed to return their cameras to school. This contrasted with the literacy strand of our project where almost all the cameras were returned with photos of out-of-school literacy (see Chapter 5 of *Improving Primary Literacy: Linking home and school*). This may reflect the greater challenge of representing mathematics on camera, which may be more demanding than showing reading and writing. However, the children engaging in these mathematics activities were older and some may have had different attitudes to the activity. For example, Nandita's sister-in-law said that she thought Nandita may have felt too shy to show her pictures in school and that is why she did not return the camera. Nandita herself said that she lost the camera.

The teachers were very interested in the photographs. Nadia's teacher described the objectives of the activity:

The idea was to see the children in action basically doing maths – in their own environment, doing things they do, and see what they think of as maths, you know, activities with their parents or brothers and sisters, playing games, or going shopping, which I thought was a nice idea actually. And that was popular.

In Ryan's class, the teacher added the album to the classroom book collection and children often spent time looking through it:

Quite often I'll see it out on the desk where somebody's got it out and had a look at it.

She noted the way the activity functioned as a shared activity for all the children and brought the class together:

I think it just sort of got them to see . . . well they got to see their friends and all their classmates, you know, at home doing things and they're all involved in this activity together. They were all part of it and it was . . . they liked seeing each other, sharing the

continued

> photos, and they were all doing similar things. . . . And it just sort of . . . I guess it sort of brought them . . . in a way it was a whole-class shared experience, so it sort of brought them together in that way.
>
> Saqib's teacher explained the way she found the photographs helpful during mathematics lessons, extending their use beyond the simple activity of creating a display or an album:
>
> > When they brought the photographs in, I think they were quite a big . . . they were a big thing for me because they showed . . . gave me an insight into their homes and actually made me think of . . . um . . . yes, you know when you have a maths lesson in class, say of weighing scales, whatever, and you talk about maths at home and children tend to sort of . . . 'Oh Miss' . . . they sit there and you're thinking, you know, you're trying to draw it out of them and then you have these pictures where they are actually using maths at home, and you can see it.

The reference to Nandita's shyness reminds us that children may have different levels of comfort about bringing aspects of home into school – about making the private public. Some children may be concerned as to how their peers will respond to the images, particularly where discontinuities may be revealed between their home and school identities. It is important that teachers lay down ground rules of respect for the photographs and the content they portray. It is also helpful if children can look through their pictures privately before they are used in class so that they can decide which ones they are happy to share. Schools may also wish to send the photos home so that parents can see them before they are used and remove any they do not want to share or have on public display. If digital cameras are used, the selection of pictures can be edited before the camera is returned to school.

Activity 5.2 Using games to link home and school

As we saw in Chapter 3, one place where mathematics is typically found out of school is in the playing of games. These can take many forms, including board games like Monopoly, table-top games like Carrom, or made-up games like 'Kerbs'. They can involve a wide range of mathematics, including different types of calculation, money exchange, logic, understandings of shape and space, and intuitions about probability and chance. Encouraging children to bring in games from home and play them in school allows them the opportunity to demonstrate and share the knowledge they have developed in connection with their game-playing. This may not just be in terms of the mathematics they are using but also concerned with rather different aspects, including social interaction and strategy development.

Playing games can have a number of benefits for learning mathematics:

- The mathematics is purposeful and used in situations that are meaningful for the child.
- Games are motivating and can provide a context in which an increased amount of calculation may be undertaken.
- Discussion within the game situation can lead children to greater communication about mathematics.
- Games often promote the use of mental methods.
- Games may support children in working at a level that is higher than usual and not restricted by expectation.
- Children's thinking may be made apparent in the course of their game-playing which can provide a helpful context for assessment.

There is much to be said, then, for encouraging game-playing more widely in the school context.

Using games – what we did

We used games in a number of different ways to link home and school, such as the following:

- Children brought games into school from home and played them in class.
- Games were a central activity in an after-school maths club.
- Several of the activities in the home–school folder (see Chapter 4) or set for homework were in the form of games.
- The parents who visited their EAL children in class (see Chapter 4) made mathematical games and played them with their children.

The games used in the last two activities were specifically designed to relate to, and complement, the topics the children were encountering in their mathematics lessons at the time. Games included imaginary shopping sprees, with particular conditions on how to spend the money, tactical games for two people in which strategies could be developed, and games to practise basic skills, such as colouring-in sections of pictures based on answers to calculations, so that the completed colouring revealed a hidden design.

Making games related to particular topics can involve a lot of work. One way of making a small number of games go further is to ask children to work in pairs as a single player. That way, more children can play with the same number of games. This mode of organisation has the added benefit of promoting discussion, often mathematical in content, as each pair of children talks about how to proceed. Where games are sent home in a home–school folder or as a homework task, making or assembling the game can be included as part of the activity.

Our experience – what people said about using games

Playing games from home in school

Olivia took in a game of Monopoly and thought it was great fun to be able to play it in school. She felt it was a good idea because it helped with motivation for mathematics (although she didn't actually need this herself):

> Yes [it's a good idea] because it's just another way of learning maths, but it's . . . well I do enjoy maths . . . but for some people it's a fun way. It's kind of a game, but it's still doing maths, like just a subject as well.

Olivia's teacher felt it was an 'excellent' activity and reported no problems with it:

> They were allowed to bring in games but they all had to have a maths relationship in some way . . . it was that . . . trying to get home into school and what did they think was maths. . . . It was very successful, they all bought in very nice games and they all played very nicely together.

continued

Games at the after-school maths club

The emphasis at the maths club was also on fun. The majority of the participants were girls, which the teacher found disappointing, but the club clashed with a cricket club and a drama club held on the same day. (Saqib said that he had to attend Mosque after school.) Leena usually attended the drama club but went to the maths club on two occasions when the drama club was cancelled. She said she was surprised at how much fun it had been. She said she didn't usually play board games but she got interested in them through the club. Children may find it difficult to envisage what a maths club might entail, so it could be useful to give children a taster of typical club activities before a club starts up so that children have realistic expectations as to what might be involved.

Leena's teacher highlighted the usefulness of the club and the games-playing as a context for finding out more about the children's capabilities:

> They've been having fun, they've been enjoying it . . . and they've learnt some really good games. [I've noticed] some girls . . . like Ruby is still sort of counting in her head, she's sort of like . . . she starts to rock her head as she counts, and it just goes to show that what we've been teaching or learning in class that day in maths, she's just not taking it on, she's still, you know, doing 'ta te ta te' – I can always hear that when she's counting and she's struggling with it.

Games as an activity sent home

When activities were sent home in the form of games they tended to be well received. Olivia's classmate Luke told us of a game he played based on fairground rides:

> The teacher gave it and I was pretty pleased because it was about a fairground and it included money, about six – no thirty – pounds and you had to spend it on fairground rides. . . . Mum and Dad and my brother, we all played it together, and my dog was very excited, and she laid under the table and watched us play it. . . . I did like that.

If making the game is included in the activity, steps need to be taken to ensure that children have the resources to undertake the activity. Farah said that they were unable to play one game because they had to cut it out and stick it on card. She said she had scissors and glue at home but did not have any card. It may be helpful in some cases to include 'making packs', which contain any resources needed.

Parents making and playing games at school

As we saw in Chapter 4, the EAL mothers at Ryan's school visited their children's mathematics class on the first Wednesday of the month. Getting the mothers to make mathematics games worked well as an activity because it gave them something to do as they listened to the lesson. They also joined the children in groups and played the games with them. This was an effective way of getting them to feel involved in the children's learning, with the group situation allowing them to contribute to the extent that they felt comfortable. The EMAS teacher said that seeing the children using the games had had an impact on her thinking and that it was her intention to include more games and more practical activities in the children's mathematics learning in the future:

> I think sometimes it's too dry and it turns children off, and if they can see that you can play with it . . . next year I would certainly try to include more practical things and games.

continued

Figure 5.3 Parents playing a maths game at school

The activity of making and playing a mathematics game (sent from school) at home can be extended to include designing the game. This allows children to include and demonstrate their knowledge of out-of-school mathematics in the content and rules they create. It may be helpful to begin with a fairly structured approach at first, where children are given an idea which they can then embellish.

In Nadia's class, the children each made a game at school which they then finished off at home. It was called 'Spend, Spend, Spend' and the idea of the game was to get rid of your money as quickly as possible. The children could decide how difficult they made the game according to the amount of money they gave to players to start with, the costs they chose for items and the spending rules they invented. The teacher noticed that after this activity a number of children started making games at home and bringing them into school, which had impressed him. This happened near the end of the school year so it was not possible to take the potential of children creating their own games any further but it was something the teacher was keen to pursue the following year.

Activity 5.3 Creating and using maths trails

Another way of giving children an opportunity to use and explore mathematical knowledge embedded in their out-of-school worlds is to get them to create maths trails. These can be made at home and then brought into school to be shared and discussed. Alternatively, children can create a trail during school time, based on their knowledge of the school neighbourhood. Readers interested in this approach can find out more about existing maths trails on the web (See, for example, http://nrich.maths. org/public/viewer.php?obj_id=2579).

Creating and using maths trails – what we did

In Saqib's school we constructed a school maths trail that led the children around the school and out into its grounds. Photographs were used to establish the locations. These were printed with accompanying questions for each station in a booklet. Answers were recorded on separate sheets so that the booklets could be reused. Figure 5.4 shows two pages from the booklet.

In addition to the type of questions shown in Figure 5.4, which related to the objects belonging to this environment, there were also questions relating to the material painted on the ground in the yard. This included a '100 square', the face of an analogue 24-hour clock and a compass rose. Rajinder recalled 'We had to answer questions like – "If it's 5 o'clock

Go to the picnic tables in the covered area of the yard.
1. If 8 children can sit around each table, how many children can use these picnic tables at the same time?
2. 9 boys sit around one table and 10 girls around another. How many children need to sit around the other table for a class of 26 children all to sit down?
3. How many more picnic tables would be needed for two classes of 28 and 27 to all sit down, with no more than 8 to a table?
4. If a class of 31 wanted to sit down, with no more than 4 to a bench, how many extra chairs would they need to fetch?
5. If everyone was in your class today, would they all be able to sit on the benches, or would you need some extra chairs?
6. If each picnic table cost £220, how much more than £500 would it cost to buy three?
7. If the PTA raised £910 how many could they buy?
8. How much money would they have left over?

Figure 5.4 Pages from the school maths trail booklet

continued

Upstairs cloakroom

Look at the rails of coat hooks in the cloakroom.
1. How many hooks are on one side of the top rail?
2. How many hooks are there on one side of the bottom rail?
3. How many hooks are there altogether on the rails?
4. How many hooks are on the wall?
5. How many hooks are there altogether in the cloakroom?
6. If there are 30 children in a class, how many classes can use this cloakroom?

Look at the windows in the cloakroom.
7. What shapes are the windows?
8. How many panes of glass are used in the cloakroom windows?
9. If it costs £5 to replace each broken pane of glass, how much would it cost to replace all the windows in the cloakroom, if they were broken?
10. How much change would there be from £100?

Figure 5.4 continued

now what time will it be in 10 hours' time?"'. Her friend said, 'In the playground, there were some numbers and time things, and we have to try and figure out the time, what's the time now by our shadow'. Questions about these features were less authentically located, but it was hoped that this focus would help to revitalise interest in the playground paintings.

Parents were invited to come into class on a particular afternoon so that they could provide help to groups of children as they worked on the trail. At the various stations, the groups discussed the best way to tackle the questions and then recorded their answers.

A second 'family maths trail' was created for children to use in their homes, with the children getting involved in its design. In part, it was similar to the school maths trail but with questions about the children's homes rather than features of the school environment. In

continued

addition, at the children's request, a section was included about their families. Questions here asked about the ages of the oldest and youngest family members, what the difference was between their ages and the average age of the family members living in the home. Other questions were concerned with the heights of family members. There were also blank pages where the children could customise the trail further to fit their circumstances and interests. There was, then, an opportunity for the children both to apply their mathematical understanding in a real world context and to pose problems that were meaningful to them.

The children completed their family maths trails at home with the involvement of their parents and other family members in some cases. The completed booklets were returned to school, which gave a further opportunity for the children to share their out-of-school knowledge with the teacher and other pupils.

It can be helpful if children are given an idea as to what a maths trail might look like by presenting them with a ready-made school-based one to follow before they are asked to work on their own out-of-school version. If such a trail uses the spaces outside the classroom, this activity will allow the children to recognise further ways in which their mathematics learning can be applied beyond the classroom walls.

Parents can be invited into school to help groups of children as they follow the school trail. This will allow them to share their own approaches to solving the mathematics problems encountered with the children, especially if it is emphasised that there is no one correct way to reach a solution. In this case, an added benefit of the activity will be the visible valuing of varied methods, especially if they are subsequently discussed with approval in the classroom.

When creating a trail for children to follow, one issue that needs to be considered is whether the same problems will be tackled by all the children or whether differentiated trails will be produced. If adults are available to accompany the children on the trail, then differentiation can be achieved by providing different degrees of help according to need, while using the same questions. A related consideration concerns decisions about grouping. Will the children work individually or in groups? If in groups, what factors will be taken into account when forming the groups? Will the children be of similar or mixed ability? Parent helpers may find particular combinations easier than others.

Consideration also needs to be given to the timing of the activity and the number of questions that children are likely to be able to tackle in the time. Groups of children may work through the tasks at different rates. It may be preferable to include less material and then include a more open section at the end. For example, children might be asked to time themselves doing an activity several times. Each time they repeat the activity they could be asked to work out their average time up to that point. They could also be asked to find out whether they are getting faster or slower. Groups who finish before the others will be able to complete a greater number of repetitions of the designated activity. Alternatively, once children have finished the trail they could be asked to think up extra questions of their own, which they might then swap with other children who have finished. Finally, starting children at different points on the trail will avoid traffic jams. This may be particularly desirable where close access is required at certain stations.

Our experience – what people said about the maths trails

The teacher at Saqib's school was delighted with the maths trail activity:

> It went really well – yes, they really enjoyed it. We didn't get to finish it . . . we didn't have enough time in the end, and they all wanted to finish it and I just said 'We'll come back to it another afternoon and do it and finish it off'. . . . It was a lovely sunny afternoon and we all went outside. The children had fun – they wanted to do it again, they wanted to finish off . . . they moaned because we had to go back in, and it just went really well.

She noted that children who rarely participated fully in mathematics lessons were fully engaged in the activity, actively seeking help from others when necessary rather than just passively letting other children take the initiative.

Erica's mother was one of the parents who helped with the activity. She enjoyed the occasion and showed some ingenuity in her approach to solving the problems:

> I felt it was great . . . but there was one where there was a line . . . people were making the assumption about how many centimetres and I said 'I don't think they are', and I lay down – fortunately it was a dry day – because I know I'm more or less roughly five foot, and I said 'Look . . . actually on my passport I think I'm 1.5 metres', and I said 'I know I'm one and a half metres tall, so that's one and a half metres'. . . . I think they had to do something like find where two metres was . . . and I said 'That's not right because I'm one and a half metres' – and I was really enjoying it.

Here we see some of the features often found in real-world problem-solving – testing the plausibility of solutions against other knowledge, using practical approaches and making creative use of what is available in the situation.

Many of the children enjoyed the activity. Dhanu 'got very far in it' and smiled as he recounted 'Me and my friend rushed along – it involved a lot of running around – writing down the activity, running, thinking, writing, stuff like that'. Erica, however, did not enjoy it. She was not happy with her partner:

> I thought it was rather boring, because you're like outside in your own school playground, and all you could really do is maths, and only some people found it fun anyway. . . . [I did it] with my mum and I was put with somebody in my class, but he's moved now and he wasn't here for that long, and I don't really know him. Anyway I'm normally friends with girls – because I'm a girl myself, kind of.

Her mother was aware of having to manage the social situation:

> I think Erica might have enjoyed it more if she'd had my sole attention or alternatively if she'd been with some different people, because I think it was the tension of her being in a pair with somebody who wasn't actually one of her friends – a boy as well. . . . What I do remember of that activity though was that I was quite proud of Erica that she sustained her attention . . . [but] I felt that tension was there. It wasn't annoying for me but I think it got in the way a little bit of the maths – the fact that I was trying to give equal attention to both children, and I didn't know one, and obviously the other was my daughter.

We need to recognise that when parents are invited into school to provide assistance, they are placed in a situation where they are interacting with their child in a context different from home. Both parent and child will need to find ways to handle the new situation and may need time and support to negotiate appropriate roles and ways of interacting.

continued

The children came up with a range of questions for their family maths trails. As with the school trail, the children found it a challenge to complete the whole trail, including the section of ready-made questions, in the time available. Rajinder thought it was quite hard and didn't manage all 'the endings' but she had attempted it on her own. It may be helpful to 'start small' with this kind of activity – and then return to it over time.

Several of the parents were positive about the activity. Leena's mother, for example, thought it was 'a good idea, that one – because it just asked her about her house and her family and all sorts of things'.

The observation from Leena's mother reminds us that it is the home – the goings-on that take place there and the family – that the child knows and is interested in. Helping children formulate their mathematical enquiry about this world has the potential to contribute greatly to their mathematics understanding.

Conclusions

This chapter has described some activities which successfully brought aspects of children's home life and learning into school. This is perhaps more familiar in other contexts in school – reading for example – but we found families and schools were keen to extend the idea into mathematics. Some of these activities broadened parents' views about mathematics and about where it is to be found in their and their children's everyday lives. They also provided contexts for families to share learning in a more informal way than homework usually does.

Box 5.1

Reflections on home-to-school knowledge

- What sort of knowledge is appropriate to share between home and school?
- How might teachers use this knowledge to help support children's learning?
- How might teachers choose the most appropriate activities for their school and community?
- What issues of confidentiality and privacy need to be considered? How can children's rights in this area be protected?
- Could activities be designed to help children broaden their out-of-school interests through increased awareness of their peers' interests?

Chapter 6

Home–school knowledge exchange

Benefits and challenges

In this final chapter we focus more closely on what we have termed *home–school knowledge exchange*, the idea underpinning the activities described in Chapters 4 and 5. We explain what we mean by this term, what its underlying principles are, and how they can be put into practice. We also look at some of the challenges which may be faced by teachers and other practitioners who want to put home–school knowledge exchange into practice, and at the benefits which might be gained from doing so. Readers who are familiar with our companion volume, *Improving Primary Literacy: Linking home and school*, will recognise many of the points made here. This is because they have arisen from our work in literacy as well as in mathematics. Home–school knowledge exchange has many characteristics which are independent of the subject context.

What is home–school knowledge exchange?

Although parents and teachers know much about different aspects of children's learning, this knowledge tends not to be well shared or built on. A central theme in previous chapters is that we need to bring homes and schools together more effectively, enabling parents and teachers to recognise what each has to offer. Parents have a deep and intimate knowledge about their children's out-of-school lives – how they approach learning, what motivates them and what they know and want to find out about. Similarly, teachers have a wealth of knowledge about children's learning at school and how to teach the range of subjects that make up today's curriculum. But although teachers know much about the curriculum and teaching approaches, they may not know much about children's out-of-school worlds. Similarly, although parents know a great deal about their children's home interests, skills and passions, they may know very little about the mathematics curriculum and how it is taught in school.

The Home–School Knowledge Exchange Project was inspired by the idea that it would be beneficial for parents and teachers to pool their 'funds of knowledge' (Gonzalez *et al.*, 2004) about children. We set out to devise activities in schools and homes that would result in parents' and teachers' knowledge becoming more explicit, so that it could be communicated and shared in order to enhance children's mathematics learning. The activities described in this book achieved this goal, and it became apparent that both teachers and parents can indeed develop rich insights into children's learning, and that home and school knowledge can indeed be gainfully shared.

Mathematics has a special position in that it carries both a mystique and, for some, an element of fear. As we saw in Chapter 2, some parents have bad memories of their own mathematics learning at school, and may lack the confidence to engage with their children's learning of it. They may also be worried about doing things 'the wrong way'. Teaching methods have certainly changed, as we described in Chapter

2, but this does not necessarily mean that everything a parent knows has no value. Indeed, as we saw in Chapter 3, children can often benefit from being shown different methods for doing the same mathematical calculation. We want to recognise the amount of mathematics which does go on in children's lives outside school, so that families can feel confident that they can contribute to this aspect of their children's learning.

It therefore became important, in many of our activities, that we were developing parents' understanding of how mathematics is involved in their children's everyday lives and helping them to feel confident in getting involved. This sometimes put the children into the position of being 'experts' who could act as a communication link between their parents and their teachers, helping to explain each world and the experiences they had in it to the other. So when we think of knowledge being exchanged between home and school, this exchange does not just involve parents and teachers, it also directly involves children as agents of knowledge exchange.

At this point we can identify key principles that underpin the process of exchanging knowledge between homes and schools to help children learn:

- All families – including children themselves – possess important 'funds of knowledge' which can be drawn on to enhance children's learning in school.
- Communication needs to take place in two directions, from home to school as well as from school to home.
- One size does *not* fit all – home–school knowledge exchange cannot be imposed in a uniform way. Some excellent ideas that have been tried and tested in one context may not work in other settings, so be prepared to amend and adapt the ideas in this book.
- Treat diversity amongst children and families as an opportunity and not a problem. Exploring the richness of children's home lives can be a highly motivating stimulus for learning in school, and with careful planning and classroom organisation, the multiplicity of ideas, issues and practices that emanate from thirty individuals can be shared with all.
- Recognise that, together with what parents and teachers know, children's own knowledge is core to the process of home–school knowledge exchange.

How do I do home–school knowledge exchange?

How can these principles be converted into effective practice? The following suggestions are based on our own experiences of doing home–school knowledge exchange.

Start with school-to-home activities

An important lesson we learned was that both schools and families wanted to start with school-to-home activities, like those described in Chapter 4, which help parents understand the mathematics curriculum and teaching methods. This was partly because our project was initially seen by parents as being school-led, an extension of schools' practices rather than an engagement with theirs. This perception changed over the course of the project, but it was important to recognise it at the start and to meet the needs that it presented. Parents were keen to understand how learning mathematics has changed since they were at school themselves – if they had been educated in the UK. For those who had not been, the interest in school practices here was all the stronger, as we saw in Chapter 2. Teachers wanted to help parents understand how mathematics is being taught, so that they would feel more confident in working with their children to support their school learning. We were keen to ensure the sharing of information went both ways, but we also tried to respond to the needs which were presented to us. We therefore began with activities which helped parents feel more comfortable with school mathematics, and then gradually moved on from this to broaden out the agenda to include more home-to-school activities as well.

Make the activities enjoyable

Many of the knowledge exchange activities we developed were enjoyable for the children involved and helped them to feel more positive about their engagement with mathematics. As we saw in Chapter 4, the children particularly enjoyed making videos to help their parents understand some of the mathematics they were engaging in at school. They also enjoyed the chance to be the expert for a change. For example, Nadia's classmate Bryn said:

> That was a fun thing to do when I got to be in charge of the whole thing . . . because I learned a lot more when I did that than I did when, say, I was sitting down being taught.

As we saw earlier, Bryn even tried to use this activity to persuade his teacher to make mathematics teaching more fun.

The maths trails and camera activity described in Chapter 5 were also widely enjoyed. For example, Erica's mother said about the camera activity:

> Oh, it was something different – it was fun. We were trying to think of something to do and I think that was the idea. You just get on with life and then you suddenly think, 'Ah – a mathematical opportunity' and you use it!

Making mathematics enjoyable will hopefully mean that fewer children will grow up – like some of the parents encountered in Chapter 2 – with a dislike or fear of mathematics. They might also, as Bryn suggested, learn more mathematics in the process.

Use diverse means of communicating with parents

In some of our schools there were significant numbers of children whose home language was not English. We used a range of different activities which provided different opportunities to be taken up by different families. Bilingual learning support assistants, documents in community languages, children acting as translators for their parents and groups of parents working together were all ways in which language barriers were overcome to improve communication. The key seemed to be to support the growth of parents' confidence so that they could feel part of the school and would want to get involved in its events. Confidence is very often an issue for parents, and this must be even more of an issue when a parent does not feel confident in the language the teacher is speaking.

For these parents in particular, there was a real benefit for some in activities directly targeted at them rather than their children. As we saw in Chapter 4, a regular computer club for mothers was very successful in one school, and this grew into a regular literacy session as well to support their learning of English. These activities grew out of visits to homes, with a bilingual member of school staff, so that parents became more confident in their contacts with the school.

Tailor activities to the school and community

An initiative like this needs to come at the right time for a school. It will only work well, and create the maximum impact, if teachers and parents are enthusiastic about what they can both gain from it. Small steps are often the best way to achieve big changes, and this is certainly true of anything which aims to change relationships. All involved need to feel included and confident if they are to contribute effectively.

We learned that while some successful ideas will spread round a school and community and take off of their own accord, others need nurturing. They need the commitment of the school's head and a place made for them in the school's busy agenda. So getting together to decide on priorities among a group of staff and parents may well be a very good way of helping to ensure that people's real needs are being met, rather than the needs that others may imagine they have. We did not always find that parents or teachers wanted what we imagined they would – we had to learn to listen and work to their agendas and not to impose our own. This was important in creating the partnership, which meant that teachers felt that we were supporting their development and not just pursuing our interests. We also found out about the huge value of working with the wider staff of a school and not just the teachers. Support staff can play a major role in making things happen, with their wide range of skills which are complementary to those of teachers. Above all, we found it essential to develop the activities and ideas that suit a particular teacher, school or community. They can be developed from those ideas that have worked for us, but they need to be tailored to individual circumstances and priorities.

Don't expect activities to work for all

Another important lesson we learned was that there are no 'perfect' activities just waiting to be found that will interest and engage everyone. (This should have been obvious, of course!) We found that the effectiveness of activities varied between schools, between teachers, between children and between parents. Families have various reasons for being more interested in some activities than others – such as their working arrangements, childcare and other family circumstances, level of confidence and language skills. Schools need to choose activities which target particular needs for communication, as do parents.

We also needed to accept that some activities only engaged a few parents, but that this did not make them unsuccessful. There were activities in which only a few families became involved in some schools, but these were still important both for the schools and families as a means of communicating. Often, a small-scale activity would target a particular group of families really well and so the advantages were quite disproportionate to the number of families involved. Some activities, such as the home–school jotters described in Chapter 4, were quite low key to start with. However their impact grew as families became familiar with how their children were learning through regularly receiving this information.

What are the likely challenges?

Let's look now at some of the reservations people may raise about home–school knowledge exchange – and at how they might be addressed.

'We're already doing it'

There may well be many schools and communities where activities resembling the ones described here are taking place. That is undoubtedly good news. Our experience, however, is that many parents feel that more could be done to help them understand what is happening in their children's school and that more account could be taken of their own knowledge. In addition, many parents feel increasingly cut off from their children's school learning as they move through primary school. Whatever schools are currently doing with parents, they must also keep asking whether it is really meeting the needs of the parents and the children.

'We couldn't do it with the families at our school'

In our project we worked with a wide range of different kinds of schools and communities. There were challenges presented by language issues, working parents, younger siblings and childcare issues, busy teachers, and irregular responses from homes. But none of these things prevented some valuable activities from being successful when the right approach was taken.

'It's not in the curriculum'

Home–school knowledge exchange has the potential to improve children's learning right across the curriculum. This kind of collaboration with families is at the heart of the relationships between schools and families which can make learning more effective and can therefore mean the curriculum is addressed in a more meaningful way. In the area of mathematics this is now being increasingly recognised, as we saw in Chapter 1. The recent Williams review of the Primary Mathematics curriculum (Williams, 2008) has argued strongly that parents 'cannot be ignored or sidelined but should be a critical element in any practitioners' plans for the education of children'.

'It can't be done – we're too busy'

Of course, schools and classrooms are extremely busy places. And there is no doubt that home–school knowledge exchange requires an additional commitment of time and energy on the part of teachers and assistants. But activities like the ones described here can be built into systems which then make them easier to manage. Once some of the basic structures are in place they can become part of the routine and not feel like an add-on. Moreover, many of the teachers and headteachers with whom we worked felt that the benefits they reaped from doing this more than justified the initial investment of time and energy.

'Children may not want to share their out-of-school lives'

Much of the value of home-to-school knowledge activities lies in the way in which children's out-of-school lives are brought into the classroom, allowing connections to be made between home and school learning. We found that the great majority of children appreciated this. At the same time it is important to recognise that some children may feel reluctant to share aspects of their private lives with their teachers and classmates. This reluctance should be respected, of course. However, there are strategies which can be used to make children feel less anxious about sharing, or to make sure they are involved in the activity, even if they have contributed very little themselves.

'I don't want parents to know what I get up to'

Just as some children may feel apprehensive about disclosing what goes on in their out-of-school lives, so some teachers may feel apprehensive about opening themselves up through knowledge exchange activities. This may be particularly the case where teachers already feel under pressure from some parents to do things differently. One teacher in our project talked about how she had shared her objectives with parents, only to be told by one parent that their child had already covered the planned work. While such encounters may not be easy, they do not invalidate the case for home–school knowledge exchange. Rather they point to the desirability of more widespread sharing and discussion between teachers and parents.

'It's not important'

We've argued strongly in this book that home–school knowledge exchange should be an integral part of learning mathematics. The children that we worked with certainly thought so – and were enthusiastic about involving their parents in their learning in a wide variety of ways. Often the success of activities was ensured by children getting their parents involved because they felt the activities were important.

Does home–school knowledge exchange work in other subjects?

Most of the activities we have described in earlier chapters could just as easily apply in other subjects. Our project had three main strands, which focused on literacy, numeracy and primary/secondary transfer (see Appendix for more details). There was much overlap between these three strands, and ideas from each strand informed the others. Some ideas, such as the camera activity described in Chapter 5, worked really well across all three strands. Full details of the literacy activities can be found in our companion volume, *Improving Primary Literacy: Linking home and school* (2007).

What are the likely benefits?

We have already seen in Chapters 4 and 5 some of the positive effects of individual knowledge exchange activities. Here we look at some of the wider benefits of a programme of home–school knowledge exchange, as reported by the headteachers of our project schools.

One key effect noticed was that of closer relationships between parents and schools. The headteacher of Nadia's school told us that it had been rare in the past for parents to come into school once their children were in the Junior department. However, the project activities created contexts for this to happen. She also emphasised that it was not just activities which were important, but also the raised awareness among staff through INSET sessions run in school by the project team.

Activities aimed at families where English was not the first language were particularly successful in creating a close relationship between these families and their children's schools. Taking about such families, Nadia's headteacher said:

> I think the project stimulated other parents talking amongst themselves and not seeing schools as somewhere you couldn't get involved in and become a part of. Their perceptions of school are far different today from their experiences when they were children, and I think it's given them a great insight into education and into developing that partnership.

The headteacher at Ryan's school, whose work on the project included initiatives to support the learning of parents as well as children, was enthusiastic about the knock-on benefits:

We've had the 'harder to reach' parents coming into school. We've had a couple of benefits from the project – where we've had sort of side-effects, as it were. So, the 'hard to reach' parents are now coming into school for open evenings and supporting some of our cultural or social events and, even this morning, we've had a group of parents in to our Eid assembly, who a few years ago we wouldn't have seen there. And also having the women's group now for literacy and a women's group for IT – these have sort of come out from them coming in to support children in the project, working in class. So they're not afraid to cross the threshold to come into the school, so I think some of the initiatives from the project are sort of embedded in the school. . . . It has given them the confidence and self-esteem to actually come in and speak – not only to the children – but also staff.

In Saqib's school, the appointment of a community development officer working alongside the project team had led to the use of the school buildings being developed to bring in more of the community. The headteacher of this school told us that:

We've had weddings, we've had funerals, we've had birthdays and all from the different communities. So they're getting into school a lot more in that way, and thinking of the school as a base.

One effect identified by the headteachers was that of more purposeful and engaging homework. With the increased emphasis on homework, particularly in the core subjects, there is a danger that this could be rather mechanical and dry – just done for the sake of it – and without the imagination that is so important in keeping children interested in mathematics. Headteachers felt that some of the activities developed by teachers in the project were much clearer in their purpose – to really draw on the learning that children do at home and to link it with their school learning. As the head of Nadia's school commented:

They've enjoyed having the home set tasks and being involved in doing that with their parents. I think it's been a great way forward. I can remember my daughter coming home with two pages of maths to do and it's just, 'Oh, take that home' – you know, something to keep your parents happy. These tasks have had a direct consequence on building good relationships between home and school, developing parents' understanding of maths and numeracy and benefiting the children. . . . This was purposeful, and it was embedded in a purposeful setting by the staff.

The 'uncovering' of the mystery of mathematics teaching was another important benefit. The headteachers wanted parents to feel they understood how their children were being taught and to remove some of the fear parents might have of being inadequate to support their children. Parents really enjoyed this involvement and the fact that their views were important. As the headteacher at Ryan's school commented:

Having parents in the classes – supporting, parents feeling confident enough to say, yes, we like working with the children in this maths, and we like doing the home–school tasks and being asked for their opinion. And also then they wanted to do more – 'I want to support my child'. . . . For me it was seeing the parents enjoying working with the children in class, the teachers planning to make that happen and make it a successful event and, you know, a more sort of open attitude generally.

Conclusions

This book started from two central assumptions – that children live and learn in two separate worlds, those of home and school, and that their learning will be enhanced if these two worlds are brought closer together. In the chapters which followed we have demonstrated the validity of these assumptions in the important area of mathematics. We hope that the insights we have provided into what is happening at home and at school have helped teachers and parents gain a better understanding of the way that mathematics is acquired and used in these two different contexts. We also hope that the examples we have provided of knowledge exchange activities will encourage and inspire readers to find their own ways of exchanging knowledge in order to support children's learning of mathematics, and that the outcomes are as effective, creative and enjoyable as those we have described here.

Appendix: The Home–School Knowledge Exchange Project

The Home–School Knowledge Exchange Project was funded by the Economic and Science Research Council (ESRC) between 2001 and 2005. The project was part of a large research programme called the Teaching and Learning Research Programme (TLRP). The TLRP is concerned with improving outcomes for learners in a very wide range of UK contexts across the lifecourse.

The Home–School Knowledge Exchange Project was based on the assumption that both parents and teachers have knowledge that is relevant to enhancing children's learning, but that this knowledge is often poorly communicated and under-utilised. The overall aim of the project was to develop, understand and evaluate ways in which pupil attainment and learning disposition could be enhanced by a process of knowledge exchange between parents and teachers, which also involved children themselves.

There were three strands to the project, with the following focuses:

- Developing literacy at Key Stage 1
- Developing numeracy at Key Stage 2
- Facilitating transfer between Key Stages 2 and 3.

Below we provide details of the numeracy strand of the project.

Numeracy strand: design

Within the numeracy strand, four schools actively participated in the project. In these schools the activities described in Chapters 4 and 5 were developed and put into practice (the 'action' schools). Two of the schools were in Bristol and two in Cardiff. Within each city, one school had a relatively high proportion of pupils eligible for free school meals while the other had a relatively low proportion. We tried to ensure that the schools' intakes reflected Bristol's and Cardiff's ethnic diversity.

A set of four schools matched to the action schools was also recruited to the project. These schools did not carry out any activities but provided the opportunity for quantitative comparisons to be made of the pupils' learning outcomes.

Numeracy activities

Three teacher-researchers were seconded to the project between 2001 and 2004, one for each strand. The role of the teacher researcher in the numeracy strand was to work closely with teachers and parents in the action schools, developing mathematics-related home–school knowledge exchange activities and supporting their implementation. The project team felt it was important not to impose ideas upon the participants. The first step, then, was a mapping exercise whereby the current state of home–school interchange and the knowledge exchange needs of those involved were investigated. Headteachers and teachers in the four numeracy strand action schools were interviewed, and parents were sent questionnaires (translated into home languages where appropriate) and invited to take part in discussion groups. (Some of the outcomes of this mapping are described at the start of Chapters 4 and 5.)

The numeracy teacher-researcher focused her work on one class in each of the four schools. At the beginning of the project the children in these classes were starting Year 4, and they continued to be the focus of the project's work during Year 5.

Evaluating the project's impact

Other members of the project team carried out work designed to evaluate and understand the impact of the knowledge exchange activities on the children, their families and their schools. A range of different methods was used for this.

Quantitative assessments of all the children in the action and comparison classes were carried out at the start of Year 4, the start of Year 5 and the end of Year 5. The assessments had three main components – a standardised assessment of the children's attainment in literacy and numeracy, an assessment of their learning disposition, and an assessment of their self-efficacy in numeracy. The children's attainment in literacy and numeracy was assessed using the PIPS tests produced by the CEM centre at the University of Durham. The children's learning dispositions were assessed using a junior version of the 'Effective Lifelong Learning Inventory' developed at the University of Bristol (Deakin Crick et al., 2004). The children's subject-related self-efficacy was assessed using questionnaires devised by the project.

In each action class, further exploration of a mainly qualitative nature was conducted with six 'target' families. Six pupils (a higher-attaining boy and girl, a medium-attaining boy and girl and a lower-attaining boy and girl) were chosen through stratified random selection. Their parents were invited to participate in this part of the research, mostly by phone, although a few were approached directly in the playground at school or at home. All but two agreed, and reserves were approached in these cases. Interviews with the parents and children in the target families were used to explore thoughts and feelings about mathematics and to monitor responses to the knowledge exchange activities retrospectively. The final set of interviews included the use of photographs taken during the activities to prompt stimulated recall. The families also made videos of numeracy events taking place at home, and the target pupils were observed in mathematics lessons at school.

More prolonged and intensive explorations were pursued with a number of families selected from amongst the targets. These case studies allowed a more detailed investigation with those involved. A variety of techniques was used here, including diaries made by the participants (both written and photographic), videos, observation, informal chats, and drawing and model-making with some of the children. The accounts given in Chapters 2 and 3 of mathematics learning at home and at school are based on some of this case study data.

During the course of the project, teachers and headteachers were interviewed individually, and informal discussions were also held from time to time. The interviews with the teachers included their views about mathematics learning and teaching, their feelings about involving parents, their responses to the activities and their appraisals of the target children. The sustainability of knowledge exchange activities was a particular feature of the discussions with headteachers.

Further information

Further information about the Home–School Knowledge Exchange Project can be found at http://www.tlrp.org/proj/phase11/phase2e.html

Further information about the Teaching and Learning Research Programme can be found at http://www.tlrp.org

References

Baker, D., Street, B. and Tomlin, A. (2003) 'Mathematics as social: understanding relationships between home and school numeracy practices', *For the Learning of Mathematics*, 23(3): 11–15.

DCSF (2008) *Statutory Framework for the Early Years Foundation Stage*, Nottingham: DCSF Publications.

Deakin Crick, R., Broadfoot, P. and Claxton, G. (2004) 'Developing an effective lifelong learning inventory: the ELLI project', *Assessment in Education*, 11: 248–272.

DfES (2008) *Primary Framework for Mathematics*. Online. Available at www.standards.dfes. gov.uk/primaryframeworks/

Feiler, A., Andrews, J., Greenhough, P., Hughes, M., Johnson, D., Scanlan, M. and Yee, W.C. (2007) *Improving Primary Literacy: Linking home and school*, London: Routledge.

Gonzalez, N., Moll, L. and Amanti, C. (eds) (2004) *Funds of Knowledge: Theorizing practices in households and classrooms*, Philadelphia: Lawrence Erlbaum.

Hughes, M. and Greenhough, P. (2003a) 'Learning from homework: a case study'. In L. Poulson and M. Wallace (eds) *Learning to Read Critically in Teaching and Learning*, 85–109. London: Sage.

Hughes, M. and Greenhough, P. (2003b) 'How can homework help learning?' *Topic 29*, NFER.

Jones, D. (2002) 'National numeracy initiatives in England and Wales: a comparative study of policy', *Curriculum Journal*, 13(1): 5–23.

Marsh, J. (2003) 'One-way traffic? Connections between literacy practices at home and in the nursery', *British Educational Research Journal*, 29: 369–382.

Merttens, R. and Vass, J. (1990) *Sharing Maths Cultures: IMPACT, Inventing Maths for Parents and Children and Teachers*, London: Routledge.

Ocean Mathematics Project (2008) Online. Available at www.ocean-maths.org.uk

Williams, Sir P. (2008) *Review of Mathematics Teaching in Primary Schools and Early Years Settings*, Nottingham: DCSF Publications.

Index

210951